SEXUALITY:
THE SACRED JOURNEY

SEXUALITY:
THE SACRED JOURNEY

An Awakening to Ecstasy

MARINA RAYE

EDITED BY CHARLIE OAKWIND

ACTION PRESS.

First printing 1994

Published by Action Press
P.O. Box 6250, Colorado Springs, Colorado 80934

Cover art copyright ©1993 by Charles Frizzell
First Edition

This book is autobiographical. However, some names and other identifying details have been changed to protect the privacy of the individuals involved.

ISBN: 1-878010-01-8

Printed in the United States of America

OTHER BOOKS BY MARINA RAYE

Do You Have an Owner's Manual for Your Brain?

Brainware: The Workbook

Sexuality: The Sacred Journey
Quotes

Note to the Reader: The Journey of Sacred Sexuality encompasses all dimensions of our being, leading us to a deeper experience of the sacredness of all life.

Most of us have been loving at ten percent of our potential.

We need to stop looking for the perfect mate to fulfill us and focus on loving ourselves.

When I encourage you to find the sacred gift in your woundedness, I am *not* excusing the perverted behavior of your abusers. They are guilty of violating your innocence and must be held accountable for their actions.

Introduction: Sacred Sexuality is the final frontier of awakening to our wholeness.

Chapter 2: As children we were programmed through fear and intimidation, which caused us to quickly forget our true identity.

The sacrament of sexuality is a profound way to experience oneness with the divine in ourselves and in our mate.

When we break free from the bondage of our past, we will remember that paradise is within the beauty of our souls.

Chapter 3: Being raised in a dysfunctional family is a common bond most of us share.

(More quotes on page 243)

To the Inner Soulmate, the harmony of the feminine and masculine in each of us. May your awakening assist in the healing of our Earth family.

About the Author

If you envisioned courage, creativity, love, enthusiasm, integrity, involvement, intellect, and action, you would be seeing Marina Raye, best-selling author of *Do You Have an Owner's Manual for Your Brain?* Her books, lectures, and workshops are alive, impactful, and empowering — they transform lives.

Marina was born in Central Africa, the third child of fundamentalist Christian missionaries. She spent the first ten years of her life in a tropical paradise, observing the manipulation and domination of native people by organized fundamentalist religion. She has retained the gentle spirit of a true native.

Marina's courage has never been tested more fully than with the writing of this book. She has written her sexual life story, including her religious and sexual abuse, her sexual frustrations and sexual addiction, and ultimately, her insights into Sacred Sexuality. By accepting her suggestions, you, too, can awaken to ecstasy through your healing journey of Sacred Sexuality.

Marina's home is in the Rocky Mountains of Colorado. She has a Master's degree in counseling psychology and is president of High Performance Training, Inc. She travels throughout the United States and the world presenting workshops and lectures. She is an accomplished musician whose favorite musical instrument is the Native American flute. Marina is love in action!

Charlie Oakwind, Editor

Our deepest pain, particularly our psychosexual woundedness, can become our sacred gift. By working through my own abuse and assisting others in their healing, I have redefined our woundedness as our sacred teacher of forgiveness and love. When we recognize our abuse, process our rage, and release our pain, we will no longer be victims of our past. We will be free to embrace our journey of Sacred Sexuality.

Contents

Note to the Reader

Have you ever wondered after making love, Is that all there is? Have you yearned for deeper intimacy with your mate? Have you experienced lovemaking that touched the core of your being, and then wondered afterward how to recapture the oneness and the ecstasy of that moment? Have you felt sexually inhibited by programming of shame, guilt, and fear? Are you recovering from sexual abuse or sexual addiction? If you answered yes to one or more of these questions, you are ready to experience your journey of Sacred Sexuality.

My use of the term *sacred* has no reference to organized religion, which implies a separation between heaven and earth, spirit and body. Sacred Sexuality is the merging of heaven and earth, spirit and body. It involves seeing the big picture as well as the little picture, experiencing ourselves and our mate as divine and human at the same time. When we embrace our wholeness, we can recognize our capacity for expressing love as multidimensional beings. We can celebrate sex as a holy sacrament.

Read this book with a beginner's mind. Allow my story to stimulate your understanding of the sacred gifts you have received from your own sexual experiences. I encourage you to use a writing journal to record the insights you receive which will help you to heal your woundedness and empower you as a sacred, sexual being. If you experience resistance, welcome it. Resistance is often denial or fear programming that is ready to be released.

Our deepest pain, particularly our psychosexual

woundedness, can become our sacred gift. By working through my own abuse and assisting others in their healing, I have redefined our woundedness as our sacred teacher of forgiveness and love. When we recognize our abuse, process our rage, and release our pain, we will no longer be victims of our past. We will be free to embrace our journey of Sacred Sexuality.

When I encourage you to find the sacred gift in your woundedness, I am *not* excusing the perverted behavior of your abusers. They are guilty of violating your innocence and must be held accountable for their actions.

Δ Δ Δ

The technology in this book has been used in my workshops with thousands of people to heal their shame, guilt, and fear programming about sex, to understand their woundedness as their sacred gift, and to awaken to ecstasy. I integrate information and tools from Neuro-Linguistic Programming, erotic-spiritual Tantric and Taoist practices, Native American Spirituality, the study of the Sacred Feminine, and other teachings that have helped me to reawaken to my Sacred Sexuality. I perceive my role as that of a midwife for the rapid transformation occurring on Planet Earth. We are currently experiencing the death throes of the paradigm that has controlled our sexuality through shame, guilt, and fear. My intent is to share a journey that will help to birth a new paradigm of sacred sexual partnership.

This story is written for men as well as women. I honor my brothers who have the courage to undertake the journey of Sacred Sexuality. As men face their fears and begin to talk openly about their woundedness, they are opening their hearts to fully experience their emotions. Our emotions are the pathway to a deeper experience of our spirituality and our sexuality. To the extent that we deny our emotions, we deny our spirits and our bodies.

I honor my sisters for the empowerment work they

are doing in healing their woundedness and bringing the sacred back into their lives. The women's spirituality movement has led us to identify with our feminine power and to live authentically.

I respect all sexual preferences. Sacred Sexuality is a journey available to anyone who chooses to experience love at the level of the sacred.

I have been bluntly honest in sharing the details of my sexual learning experiences. My intent is not to titillate but to stimulate you to examine your experiences for their sacred gifts. My sexual addiction occurred before the time when AIDS became a known threat. I advocate sharing the journey of Sacred Sexuality in a committed relationship in which you practice safe sex. I hope that the story of my sexual and spiritual healing and the healing methods that I share will inspire you on your journey of Sacred Sexuality.

No book contains all the answers to a richer, fuller experience of your sexuality. The answers are in your remembering yourself as a spiritual being gifted with a human body. It is time to awaken from the historical illusion that our bodily functions, particularly sex, are shameful acts. Our body is the temple of the Divine. Our sexuality is a sacred path that, when followed with love and respect, will lead us to a place of expanded spiritual awareness.

It is also time to take back our projections of the ideal man or ideal woman that we have placed on our mates. Our expectations of romantic love have kept most of us dissatisfied and frustrated. We need to stop looking for the perfect mate to fulfill us and focus on loving ourselves. Our journey into wholeness will introduce the concept of the Inner Soulmate, the harmony of feminine and masculine in each of us. The inner journey opens us to our place of power, that place where we experience our oneness with all.

Most of us have been loving at ten percent of our

potential. We have forgotten that ecstasy is our birthright. We must experience ecstasy within ourselves, or we will never be able to share it with another. When we resacralize our sexuality, we can experience ecstasy in every aspect of our lives — from our relationship with ourselves as whole beings to our relationship with our mate, from our inner spiritual development to following our bliss in our life's work, from our interaction with our human family to the way we honor our Mother, the Earth. The journey of Sacred Sexuality encompasses all dimensions of our being, leading us to a deeper experience of the sacredness of all life.

The time to release sexual shame, guilt, and fear is now. The time to delight in the sanctity of your body is now. The time to be fully, gloriously alive is now. You deserve Sacred Sexuality now.

Let the celebration begin!

Marina Raye

Introduction

only undertake projects that scare me. In writing a book on sexuality, I had to face my unprocessed woundedness that had been hidden away for years, waiting to terrorize me. I also had to deal with the fear of facing the truth about my past and open myself to accept the sacred gift in each experience.

My disclosure of my sexual history will undoubtedly cause pain and misunderstanding for my family of origin. That is a risk I must take. My intent is to share my lessons about sexuality, love, and ecstasy with openness and vulnerability, and to share my discoveries of sexual truths as a light for others on their sacred journey back to themselves. During this process I have laughed, cried, and relived the emotions of my experiences, from rage to joy, from sadness to understanding, from fear to love. My experiences and those of many people in my workshops have given me hope that we can rid our lives of the shame, guilt, and fear associated with sexuality. We can heal our woundedness and embrace our wholeness through the journey of Sacred Sexuality.

We have been living in the sexual Dark Ages. Our techno-based society has excelled in matters of the intellect while adhering to antiquated and toxic beliefs about the human body, especially our sexuality. Most of us are recovering from the shame, guilt, and fear programming of our childhood. Some of us suffered sexual abuse from those who used sexuality as a form of manipulation, domination, and the projection of their shame, guilt, and fear programming. The cycle of abuse must be broken. This book offers a path out of the sexual

Dark Ages — the journey of Sacred Sexuality.

The journey we will share begins in Zaire, Africa, the country of my birth. My parents were fundamentalist Christian missionaries, representing a patriarchal religion that attempted to program the native people to accept the white man's religion. The richness of the sacred traditions of the native people, and the lush, tropical surroundings profoundly affected the early years of my journey. **The Journey from Innocence** was filled with paradox. The programming of salvation psychology taught me that I was born a sinner and that I should treat my body and my sexuality as shameful and sinful. The free-spirited natives had no such hangups. They embraced life with childlike innocence, comfortable with their sexuality as they lived in harmony with all of life in the untamed jungle. It was in Africa that I bonded with the Earth and had my first interest in what I now call Sacred Sexuality.

My innocence was violated when I was fourteen in an act of rape that I buried in shame and denial for many years. This sacred journey is a story for anyone who has suffered from psychological and physical abuse. It is also for those who have suffered because of the stereotypical sexual programming of shame, guilt, and fear. It is about the healing process of discovering who we are apart from the limitations placed upon us by many dysfunctional systems: family, religion, education, government, society, and by individuals who have demanded our obedience. As I searched for wholeness, I studied many religions, including Eastern philosophies and Native American Spirituality. My education led me to study psychology, mythology, metaphysics, holistic healing, and music, opening new vistas into the hidden treasures within the human soul.

This journey has also led me to heal my woundedness from sexual abuse and sexual addiction. During the **Journey Through Hell**, I abused my sexuality to the extent that sex became a drug to anesthetize me from loneliness and pain. My journey has helped me to accept total responsibility for my choices and to release the need to feel like a victim. It has also helped me to identify with the loneliness and pain that is a frequent occurrence for most of us living in a world of existential despair. We are systematically conditioned to believe that we are separate from God, from nature, from each other, and from ourselves, especially our sexuality. This separation can lead us to attempt to find our identity and fulfillment in abusive relationships, addictive behavior, and denial of our Sacred Sexuality.

Feeling unworthy and unloved, I became calloused and jaded toward men and toward sexuality. After searching for years for my idealized projection of God-man, I became convinced that he did not exist. My divorce and the years following had left deep emotional scars, a psychosexual woundedness. Out of desperation, I gave up my dream of finding the perfect man. Sex became less important, simply an interesting diversion, as I dedicated myself to my career.

When I least expected it, the **Soulmate Journey** began, bringing my life partner, Charlie Oakwind, into my healing process. At first, I tried to sabotage our relationship because of my fear of commitment and feelings of shame and unworthiness. Charlie's love, patience, faith, and understanding never wavered as our bonding process led us through difficult challenges. We have both experienced quantum growth in the process of co-creating our lives. The highs and lows of our sexual relationship and our desire for greater intimacy have led us to explore sacred ways to deepen our expression of love.

The **Journey Home** has been one of releasing my fears and healing my woundedness. It has been an awakening to sexuality as a method of communing with the Divine, an awakening to ecstasy. It is also a time of living my dream as a spiritual teacher during this period of rapid transformation on the planet. In this section of the book, I share some of the methods that I have used for my sexual healing and to assist others on their journey. I describe the joys of Sacred Sexuality, a nurturing, meditative form of loving which moves us from genital sex to full-body orgasm.

The **Journey from Scared to Sacred Sexuality** offers a summary of the steps involved in reclaiming the ecstasy that is our birthright. Beginning with acknowledging and healing our woundedness, we release the shame, guilt, and fear so that we are free to experience our sacredness. An important step is forgiving our parents and our religion of origin, making peace with those who were the products of their own fear programming. Learning to speak the language of conscious loving, we share our needs and our emotions in sexual communication with our partner. When we no longer project our romantic ideals onto our mate, we will be free to embrace our Inner Soulmate. Thus we join our feminine and masculine energies in harmony and open ourselves to ecstasy.

Sacred Sexuality is the final frontier of awakening to our wholeness. There is a sexual revolution occurring — the true sexual revolution. Individuals are quietly reclaiming the sacredness that has been lost from the expression of sexuality for thousands of years. The journey of Sacred Sexuality introduces our soul to our body without the programming of shame, guilt, and fear. When we accept ourselves and each other as sacred, sexual beings, we transform our world into one of balance and harmony. The journey of Sacred Sexuality assists us in walking the sacred circle of life with love, joy, peace, and ecstasy!

PART ONE

JOURNEY FROM INNOCENCE

The journey of Sacred Sexuality is the process of reclaiming the lost innocence of our childhood. It involves healing our woundedness so that we can embrace the ecstasy which is our birthright.

Chapter 1

The Dark Continent

It was full moon in the African jungle. Blue-white light emanated from the moon, causing even the shadows to glow mysteriously. Palm fronds rustled in the breeze. The air was heavy with the singing of a chorus of crickets.

There would be a ceremony soon. Since sundown the drums from the nearby village had been sounding incessantly, telegraphing the message throughout the jungle. My mother found it difficult to sleep. The heathen practice of dancing to honor the moon was one of many ancient traditions that the missionaries deplored. Probably some of the recent converts to Christianity were already dressed in their ceremonial clothing with colorful beads and painted faces. Backsliders! The white woman wished that these people she had come to save would be easier to civilize. Mission work was a challenge, but she believed in her calling. It was her duty to try to save the heathen natives from their ancient spiritual traditions, to save them from going to hell.

Then she remembered the girls. Thirty native girls, ranging in age from eight to thirteen, were locked safely in their hut nearby. My mother had recently become their housemother and teacher. These girls, wrested by the missionaries from their native traditions, were cloistered in a boarding school environment. They were required to study the Bible and also received education in hygiene and child raising. When they were fourteen, they would be suitable candidates for marriage to black African Christian ministerial students.

The drums were sounding louder and closer. My mother could hear muffled singing from the village. Then she heard, "Nah, nah, nah-nah-nah," followed by the sound of rhythmic clapping. It was coming from the direction of the girls' hut. She got dressed, grabbed a flashlight, and hurried up the moonlit path, breathing heavily as she reached the door. She turned the key in the padlock, opened the door, and shone her flashlight on the forms of thirty girls, apparently asleep on their grass mats on the dirt floor.

I must have been dreaming, she thought. Too much African sun is making me imagine things. She locked the door and walked back to the simple wooden frame home she shared with her husband and children. A few minutes later she heard it again, the unmistakable sound of singing and clapping. She raced back to the girls' hut, circled it, and found what she had feared. The wooden slats on the hut's only window had been pried open, and the girls had escaped. When their lookout saw the white woman approaching, they had all quickly crawled back through the window except one twelve-year-old girl. Fesa, who was overweight, was stuck in the small window, being pulled by twenty-nine screaming, giggling girls. They had attempted to escape from their confinement to dance and sing to the full moon, as had been their ancestral custom for centuries.

As a representative of the patriarchal religion, my mother's duty was to report the incident to the mission authorities the next morning. All thirty girls were lined up and given five lashes with a whip on their bare bottoms by the senior male administrator. The punishment for disobedience was swift and heartless. Tears and wails melted quickly into compliance as the girls promised never again to participate in the heathen moon ceremony. As a young white girl, I was not aware of this incident when it occurred. I slept innocently in my bed, shielded from this clash of belief systems.

Many years later when I heard this story told by my parents, I said, "That was child abuse, Mom!"

"No, it had to be done. They had to be taught obedience for their own good."

It would be interesting to conduct a psychological study to determine how this religious abuse has affected the lives of these thirty precious souls. I am deeply saddened to have been a part of the enslavement of their minds, and I am determined to do my part to atone for such atrocities.

This story is a metaphor for the loss of innocence each of us has suffered. Although we may not have had our culture and beliefs stolen from us in such a dramatic and violent manner, we have been equally abused. We have had our innocence violated by the abuse of others or by the abuse of a condemning religion. Most of us were taught to be obedient to a system of rules that violated our free spirits. We were taught what to think and how to act so that we would conform to a religion, society, and government that controlled us through fear. We accepted hand-me-down shame and guilt about our bodies and our sexuality and learned to deny our emotions. Many of us even taught the same toxic beliefs to our children, continuing the cycle of abuse.

Awareness of our loss of innocence is the beginning of our journey of Sacred Sexuality. The ultimate challenge is to liberate ourselves from our past programming, from the fear-based precepts of salvation psychology. These precepts taught us that we were unworthy sinners and that our bodies were shameful. Fortunately, many of us are awakening to sexual wholeness. We are opening ourselves to healing and to experiencing ecstasy. Some of us are again dancing to the moon!

Δ Δ Δ

I once asked my father why Africa was referred to as the Dark Continent. He replied that it was because of its spiritual darkness and total isolation from the rest of the world. He also mentioned that the slave trading in Africa was part of its darkness. When I asked him who was responsible for the slavery, he admitted it was originally the white settlers in Africa, and later, the white people of the Americas.

My belief is that early white explorers and missionaries called this beautiful, untamed continent dark because of its unexplored vastness, and because of their prejudice against the dark-skinned people whom they considered heathen and inferior. Countless acts of violence have been committed against these free-spirited people of rich culture and ancient Earth wisdom, all committed in the name of religion and progress. Although my parents went to Africa out of a sincere desire to be of service to their God, they represented a patriarchal religion that controls and destroys through cultural annihilation and spiritual enslavement.

Modern technological society has imposed massive destruction on Planet Earth, destroying anyone and anything that stands in the way of progress. In order to return to balance, we need to listen to those who are still in touch with the Earth and the sacredness of all life. I am not trying to perpetuate the notion of the noble savage. The indigenous societies do have their share of problems. Yet many of their issues originated with the influence of the Western world and its patriarchal religions. In using the term *patriarchal,* I am referring to religions that were established and controlled by masculine-dominated principles and actions. I am not excusing women from their role in propagating the imbalance. For the past six thousand years women have cooperated with the patriarchal religions, teaching their children blind obedience to an imbalanced and punitive system.

There is a vital link between our attitude toward our bodies and toward the body of Mother Earth. That link is the shame, guilt, and fear programming which has alienated us from ourselves and from the sacredness of life. What we do to the Earth, we have done to ourselves. We can only abuse and exploit that which we feel separate from. Our healing process involves reawakening to the sacredness of all life. When we once again honor our sexuality as sacred, we will naturally walk in harmony with all life on our Earth home.

When I was in Rio de Janeiro at the 1992 Earth Summit, the stars of the people's revolution for the environment were the indigenous people. Elders who honor the sacred ways, who know how to walk the Earth in harmony, attended the Global Forum as teachers of the ancient traditions.

It was in Rio that I became friends with Winnifred Awosika, a tribal chief from Ikeja, Nigeria. Although our skin coloring is different, our backgrounds are amazingly similar. Winnifred went to a mission school and was programmed to believe in the salvation psychology of a fundamentalist Christian doctrine. After many years of practicing this borrowed religion, she began to question its fear-based precepts. This highly educated woman of power returned to her ancient tribal spirituality. She is the founder and director of her own high school and college in Nigeria where young people are taught the sacred ways of their ancestors in conjunction with a high-quality academic education.

I commended Winnifred for taking a step backwards into the future. Youth who are taught to understand and respect the sacred ways will remain connected to their hearts and to the Earth. When we have advanced technology without the balance of the heart, we are in grave danger of destroying the sustainability of our Earth home.

One of the Native American elders from Northern Canada spoke passionately at the Global Forum in Rio, urging us to find a clean place on the Earth, fall down upon our knees, and beg for forgiveness. I suggest that we also need to touch our naked bodies lovingly, reverently, and beg for forgiveness. We need to experience our sexuality as sacred, not to transcend the body, but to treasure it as the temple of the Divine.

The rich, spiritual traditions of the Dark Continent of Africa are a source of light which can illuminate our sacred journey into sexual wholeness. Although I was shielded from the practices of African spirituality as a child, I feel fortunate to have been able to bond with the true spirit of Africa. It was the first major step in my journey of Sacred Sexuality.

Chapter 2

Where Do Babies Come from, Mama?

Were you denied vital sexual information as a child? Were the myths of Santa Claus, the Tooth Fairy, the Easter Bunny, and the stork carefully perpetuated as truth, while a cloak of silence surrounded the subject of sexuality? Was nudity considered embarrassing? Did you feel as though God were sitting on a white cloud monitoring your sexual thoughts and actions? Did you enter puberty with more ignorance than innocence? Did you teach your children the same hand-me-down shame, guilt, and fear that you received from your parents? We have been living in the Dark Ages of sexuality. It is time to step into the light.

Δ Δ Δ

"Where do babies come from, Mama?" I was seven years old and had been pestering my mother for information. She gave me her standard response, "When a man and woman live together as man and wife, Marina. Now get on with your schoolwork." End of subject. I imagined a man and a woman brushing their teeth in the morning, fixing breakfast, and drinking coffee together, and wondered how these activities could possibly make babies. We were isolated in the heart of Africa with no television, radio, or newspapers. The only other little white girl my age on the mission compound had been sent with her older sisters to boarding school. There was no one to answer my question, Where do babies come from, Mama?

I crawled into my mosquito-net canopied bed, still pondering the same question. How was I going to find out about babies so that I could someday have my own? It would be months before my brother and sister returned from boarding school for summer vacation. I could not wait that long. I drifted off to sleep and experienced the following dream:

I was in a world of lush, tropical beauty. A sparkling stream lilted over rocks and boulders, cascading over a tumultuous waterfall. The sunlight filtered the spray into dancing rainbows that beckoned me closer. I moved slowly toward the sounds of voices and laughter, then stopped suddenly. A woman and a man were there, beautiful naked bodies glistening from the water's spray. They stood next to the waterfall, their hair dampened into ringlets, splashing each other playfully.

I watched from behind a tree as they began to caress each other's bodies. I was transfixed as I watched the man gently kiss the woman's erect nipples. He treated her with love and respect, as though her body was sacred. Then he began to run his hands slowly over her smooth buttocks and thighs. She lay down on a blanket beside the stream while he covered her body with kisses, lingering to honor her sacred space with his tongue. She moaned softly, moving her body in a slow, undulating rhythm. Then he lay down on the blanket beside her. She first kissed him passionately on his lips. Then she began licking and kissing his body, using her hands and mouth to massage his erection. She sucked and stroked him in a way that honored his sacredness. She lowered

her body onto his, guiding his hardness into her open-
ing. They began to move slowly in unison, expressing
their pleasure with sighs and moans ...

My dream vision faded as I drifted into a deep sleep.
I awoke the next morning in a state of disbelief, as I
remembered what I had dreamed. There had been no
guilt, shame, or fear in what I had observed. My childhood innocence knew that what the lovers had shared
was sacred, yet my religious programming had led me
to believe that naked bodies were shameful, not sacred.
Having never observed any signs of sexual passion in
my parents' relationship, I told myself that such
delights belonged only in dreams and still wondered
where babies came from.

That childhood dream experience remains as vivid
today as when I was seven years old. I can close my
eyes and return to my Dreamtime at any moment. It
represents the exquisite blend of the sacred with sexuality that I have searched for in my own experiences.
How did I have such a dream? My parents did not allow
me to be alone with the native people. Living a totally
protected life with no outside influences from media or
friends, I had no conscious memory of two people making love. Life was a mystery. Life was innocence. Life
was also obedience.

Δ Δ Δ

For most of us, childhood was a time in which we
were programmed to accept the limiting beliefs of our
parents and their religion, and the behavioral patterns
of society's norms. It is as though we were given a tran-
quilizer each day along with our vitamins so that we
would be good little girls and boys, obedient to all that
we were taught. Then we spend much of our adulthood
attempting to dehypnotize ourselves from our shame,
guilt, and fear programming.

There is a much-loved story of a four-year-old boy
who had a newborn baby sister. He asked his mother if

he could speak with his sister alone. She questioned him as to his reasons, and he simply replied, "I need to ask her something. Please, Mommy."

His mother agreed to his request but left the door open and listened. He spoke softly at her cribside, "Baby sister, please tell me again about God — I'm starting to forget."

My belief is that we come from Spirit and that we are born with complete cellular encoding of the wisdom of the universe. We are beautiful, wise, luminous beings who have chosen to live in human form so that we may learn the lessons that are necessary for our evolution. As children we were programmed through fear and intimidation, which caused us to quickly forget our true identity. Thus we obediently accepted from our parents and our religion the message that sex was sinful. Without understanding why, we felt shame and guilt about our body, which we were taught was totally separate from our spirit.

The term *sacrament* refers to that which is sacred or holy, a means of communing with the Divine. The sacrament of sexuality is a profound way to experience oneness with the divine in ourselves and in our mate. I received the opposite message in my upbringing as the daughter of missionaries in Central Africa. My parents' discomfort with my questions about sexuality and the human body led me to believe that sex was a forbidden subject. Those who enjoyed their bodies were sinning in the eyes of God.

My parents are from Holland, where they were taught the rigidly conservative principles of the Dutch Reformed Church. After extensive religious training, they became missionaries with a strict fundamentalist organization headquartered in England. They had been programmed to believe that anything to do with the body was too nasty and shameful to discuss. My mother referred to genitals as "down there," and when I began menstruating, she called it my *gedoetje,* the Dutch word for "thing." I was never given any basic information about sex, which led to my being sexually violated as a young teenager.

Conversely, the native people were completely comfortable with their bodies, dressing in minimal clothing of waist wraps and headdresses. When these free spirits, who practiced an Earth religion, were converted to Christianity, they would then clothe themselves in the style of the white man. They had to vow to forsake the ritualistic path of their ancestors. Thus they took on the shame, guilt, and fear programming of salvation psychology. Surrounded by conflicting belief systems, I wondered what was wrong with these beautiful native people that they had to be just like the whites.

The childlike wisdom of my Dreamtime had brought the answer to my questions about sexuality, yet it would be years before I would recognize the truth. The journey of Sacred Sexuality is the process of reclaiming the lost innocence of our childhood. It involves healing our woundedness so that we can embrace the ecstasy which is our birthright. Paradise was never lost, simply hidden from us by shame, guilt, and fear programming. When we break free from the bondage of our past, we will remember that paradise is within the beauty of our souls.

Chapter 3

Abandonment

Have you ever felt abandoned? Have you ever felt so lonely that you did not care if you lived or died? Have you felt rejected for being too expansive, too free-spirited, or too loving?

Most of us have painful memories of abandonment. Our parents and our religion taught us to believe that we were unworthy. The expression, Children are to be seen and not heard, is a typical example of the devaluation of the formative years. A parent's disciplinary comment such as, Go to your room, left us feeling guilty and undeserving of love. Abandonment was our punishment for being alive. These experiences can cause a woundedness that inhibits our entering fully into life. We withdraw into our protective armor where we can remain safe from pain and from ecstasy. It is vital to our journey of Sacred Sexuality that we heal our perception of our woundedness.

Δ Δ Δ

My father had a gentleness which would turn to harsh, Godly wrath when provoked. Although he reprimanded me verbally, he spanked me only once. My mother, however, was generous with her hair brush and fly-swatter spankings as punishment for disobedience.

I was five years old, and my brother, Henry, was tickling me during morning prayers. I started giggling and was quickly silenced by Dad's angry stare. After prayers, he told me to go to my room and that he would spank me when he returned from an errand. My brother advised me to place one of my *Little Golden Books* in my panties against my buttocks for protection. An hour later I received a Godly spanking. Book discovered, Dad told to me remove it, and I received extra punishment for deception. This punishment intimidated me into believing that religion was deadly serious and that I needed to quell my exuberant spirit. Being good and obedient seemed my only option.

My parents practiced one of the most conservative and rigid of religious dogmas. I was taught that I was a worthless sinner. "Amazing grace, how sweet the sound, that saved a wretch like me," are words that remain in my memory as a symbol of my childhood religious programming. I would be condemned to hellfire and damnation unless I chose atonement for my sins through the blood of Jesus Christ.

Salvation psychology is a heavy doctrine to cut your teeth on. I can remember my prayers as a child, begging God for forgiveness, repeating over and over, "Please, please, please, forgive me." Yet I had to be programmed to know what my sins were. Sins were even categorized as those of commission and of omission — those things you did or even thought about, and those things you neglected to do. I was damned if I did and damned if I didn't. This negative conditioning caused reaction patterns of shame, guilt, and fear that lasted well into my adult years. I was haunted by fear of the wrath of God and by a deep sense of unworthiness. I have chosen to release these toxic beliefs and reimprint my brain with love for myself and my worthiness of joy, love, and especially, Sacred Sexuality.

A religion that teaches an innocent, creative child obedience by forcing her into a strict mold of pious behavior and harsh expectations is abusive. As the daughter of missionaries, I was expected to be an exemplary child and to model perfect behavior, another form of religious abuse. I was destined to fail, no matter how hard I tried to be good. And try to be good, I did. I was so good that I became an enabler personality. My religion taught me that it was an honor to turn the other cheek to people who mistreated me, as long as I was acting in the name of Jesus.

My older sister, Joan, fared much worse than I. Her story is the ultimate example of religious abuse. The regulations of my parents' sponsoring organization, ultraconservative fundamentalists, forbade married couples to have children during missionary service. Living conditions were primitive and not conducive to caring for a baby. There were ulterior motives, however. The mission directors were concerned that children would be a distraction, that a mother would spend less time doing mission work, reducing her effectiveness for God.

During the first six months of their marriage, my parents practiced celibacy because of their fear of breaking mission rules. Once they began having intercourse, they utilized the rhythm method of birth control. It eventually failed, and my mother conceived. Due to health complications, she had to leave Africa to go to London during the sixth month of her pregnancy. After she gave birth to my sister, she was told by the director of her sponsoring mission that she would have to leave her first-born in England. Mom's other choice was to be separated from Dad indefinitely.

I have tried to imagine my mother's anguish, holding her beautiful newborn and being ordered to choose between her child and her husband. She stayed in England as long as she dared and finally left her baby of seven months in a British children's home. Mom left

19

her heart behind in the process. Three years later World War II began, prohibiting my parents from returning to England to get Joan, as they had originally planned. It was nine heartbreaking years before my sister was reunited with our family.

My healing journey has given me understanding of the greatest sorrow of my mother's life. I have always wondered why Mom had such a protective shell around her, and how she could be so blunt and heartless in her criticism of me. It was because she had to deny her emotions when she abandoned my sister. I have released my bitterness with recognition of the pain and guilt she has undergone. In discussing this experience, she has often said that she wished she had kidnapped her own child and returned to Africa with her.

When the war was over, Joan joined my parents, my brother, and me in Africa. She was enraged over her abandonment and traumatized by having been in London during the air raids of World War II. She did not realize that her torture was just beginning.

Joan was a bright but rebellious child, and my parents could not control her. She was always getting into trouble, failing classes in the mission boarding school or getting suspended for disciplinary reasons. When I was ten, we left Africa to immigrate to the United States, where Joan continued to cause problems. Finally, in desperation, my parents had her committed to the state mental hospital in Chattahoochee, Florida.

What followed was a crime that destroyed her free spirit. Her psychiatrist diagnosed her as schizophrenic and received my parents' permission to administer shock treatment. Although my sister is no longer institutionalized, her emotional state is unstable. She is tranquilized and obedient to the system which now owns her brain. She is the ultimate example of the abuse caused by a religion that has lost touch with its heart.

Before the last two occasions of shock therapy, Joan

got down on her knees and begged the doctor not to go through with the treatment. She cannot sleep on her back now because she will have nightmares that she is being strapped to a table to be given shock treatment. Joan's whole life has been a study in the bondage of the human soul in the name of religious obedience.

How could parents approve such torture for their daughter? They did not dare to question the doctor's authority, as they had not questioned the organization that had ordered them to abandon Joan in England. They were blindly obedient to a manipulative and punitive system. I do not blame them for their decisions. They did what they thought they had to do. In a recent discussion about leaving Joan in England, my parents said that they would have left their sponsoring organization, if they had just had the courage to question the authority of anyone who would make such inhumane policy decisions.

This story is vital to my journey because it explains the depth of mind control that can occur in the name of religion. People who surrender their free will and act from blind obedience violate the integrity of the soul. Although you may not have suffered from such radical abuse, you may have experienced abandonment and feelings of unworthiness, shame, guilt, and fear as a result of your childhood programming by your parents, religion, and society. Your woundedness can leave you bitter and haunted by terror, as in the case of my sister, whose trauma has lasted over fifty years. Or you can choose to change your perception of your woundedness and look upon each experience as a sacred teacher.

I feel a deep sadness that I raised my daughter with similar shame, guilt, and fear religious programming. She has had the courage to begin healing her woundedness and is on a path of enlightenment. I am confident that the cycle of abuse will stop with the way she will raise my future grandchildren.

21

△ △ △

Obedience lessons were administered early in my family. Mom began potty training me when I was two days old. The child-raising training she had received in England encouraged immediate disciplining of infants so that they would be as little trouble as possible to their parents. She placed a cold, stainless steel potty against my bare bottom after each feeding. I was forced out of diapers by the time I was nine months old, before I was developmentally ready. This training was a form of abuse. I needed gentle love and nurturing, not obedience to rules beginning at day two of my life! No wonder I have been plagued with bladder and kidney infections and bowel problems all my life. I was traumatized and received physiological and emotional anchoring that led to health problems in adulthood. Now that I realize the cause of my trauma, I have been able to heal much of my discomfort. Awareness is the first step in any healing process.

When I was five years old, my parents left me in a home for the elderly for three weeks while they went on an evangelism tour. When they returned, I was sitting on the front steps, my head in my hands, and tears on my face. I greeted them with disbelief. I had thought that I, too, was abandoned, that they were never going to return. My feelings of abandonment were so deep that this painful memory was buried in my subconscious for many years. Only recently has this experience surfaced, allowing me to heal the trauma.

At age six, missionary children were sent away by their parents to boarding school. The school was a long day's drive from us. The African roads were deeply rutted, and at times during the rainy season, they were impassable. My brother and sister came home only for summer vacation and a month at Christmas. Eight months out of the year, my parents relinquished their responsibilities of raising Henry and Joan by turning them over to the mission school. This plan did not work for me. I was too sick with malaria to be away from home.

I needed a great deal of nurturing as a child. My parents were too busy to have much time to spend with me. They both worked long days and many nights at their missionary duties — teaching school, seminary training, running the local post office, correspondence, translation work, paramedical duties, and traveling to outlying areas. Every two weeks, almost to the day, I would have a high malarial fever and spend a few days in bed, nursed with quinine, and games, stories, and sympathy from my workaholic parents. I was able to receive the love and nurturing that my brother and sister were denied. Disease always has a reason, although the reason is usually unconscious.

Δ Δ Δ

In the process of relating my childhood abandonment experiences to this journey of Sacred Sexuality, I realize how frequently most of us have felt abandoned. We felt abandoned when we most needed nurturing by being told to stop crying and be big boys and girls. We felt abandoned when we expressed our creativity and our efforts were criticized — we were told to stop coloring outside the lines. We felt abandoned when we chose to be unique and special, when we had our own style and were told we did not fit in. We felt abandoned when we searched for our own expression of spirituality and were ordered to conform to our parents' religion. We felt totally abandoned when we became curious about anything to do with the human body, especially our sexuality.

Being raised in a dysfunctional family is a common bond most of us share. Research has shown that ninety-seven percent of all families are dysfunctional. Adulthood is the time in which we heal ourselves from the effects of the fear-based programming of our childhood. It is deplorable that most adults teach their children the same toxic beliefs they were taught. This is especially true in the area of sexuality. As children we needed a healthy understanding and acceptance of our budding sexuality. Instead, most of us felt abandoned, and that sense of abandonment can last a lifetime.

I often wonder how this system perpetuated itself. Obedience to a punitive system continues the cycle of abuse. My prayer and my intent is that Sacred Sexuality will empower us to heal our woundedness and choose a different future for ourselves and our children. It is time to redesign the system.

Chapter 4

Childhood Lessons from Africa

A land of many contrasts, Africa provided me with childhood lessons that deeply affected my sexual experiences. I was trusting and innocent, much like the native people. I was unprepared for the harsh lessons that I would learn about life in a world dominated by masculine energy.

Δ Δ Δ

It was my fifth birthday, and all the mission children came to my house for a party. We played games and ate cake and homemade ice cream. Too soon, the party was over. Everyone went home except my friend, Timmy, and his mother.

Timmy and I decided to climb a tree, and halfway up the tree, he bit me, for no reason at all. He sank his teeth into my arm, leaving a circle of white marks. I scurried down, crying, "Mama, Mama, look what Timmy did to me!"

Mom and Timmy's mother, whom the mission children called Aunt Sally, were standing nearby, talking. When Aunt Sally saw my arm with teeth marks on it, she went over to her sulking son and bit his arm. "That will teach you what it feels like to be bitten!" Then there were two of us crying.

Mom felt so sorry for Timmy that she reached into her pocket, pulled out a piece of candy, and handed it to him, saying, "Now you can feel better."

There was no candy for me. We lived in an isolated area far from civilization, and it was rare for us to have candy. The last piece went to soothe the hurt feelings of the aggressor.

Through a series of childhood lessons, I was programmed to be submissive to those who caused pain. The message I received was, Be nice, at all costs, so that others will calm down and behave more predictably, without signs of emotion. Enable people, especially males, so they can keep their egos intact.

Another programming I received was that boys were better than girls. A son was honored because he would carry on the family name. I worshiped my brother, Henry, who is five years older than me. He was a daredevil, riding his bicycle fifty kilometers through the jungle, swimming in crocodile-infested rivers, and acting as if it were nothing special. When he came home from boarding school on vacation, I followed him around like his shadow.

My brother had special privileges because of his gender. He would receive much attention each night after dinner when he would lean back in his chair and proudly announce, "Now it's time for my most famous burp!" All conversation stopped while we laughed and applauded. Mom always rolled her eyes with a look that said, Boys will be boys. I was envious. Girls did not get to do such things.

My education was home schooling with a brilliant teacher — my mother. The enriched course of study included art, music, and mythology. I loved to read, especially the stories of the goddesses and gods. My reading provided a window into a different world from that of my parents. It opened my mind to new horizons, allowing me to travel the universe with my mythological companions. I imagined myself riding across the skies in Apollo's golden chariot, throwing thunderbolts in imitation of Zeus, possessing the wisdom of Athena, and the beauty and love of Aphrodite.

There was a magical part of me that knew I was different. A scrawny kid with long legs, hand-me-down dresses, and a pith helmet, I spent hour after hour alone in a sun-drenched land, deepening my bond with the Earth. I learned to listen and to observe carefully. The creatures recognized my love for them. I rescued and nursed many injured birds, and buried the ones who did not survive in a special ceremonial area for the winged ones. I was a true Earth child. There were few toys and dolls to entertain me. There were even fewer children with whom I was allowed to play. My parents did not consider native children appropriate playmates for me. I was alone much of the time with nature as my playground and the birds and animals as my companions.

An injured owl came to me and stayed long enough for me to accept the owl as a powerful symbol in my life. It represents transformation, wisdom, and discernment. Many Native American people will not touch owl feathers. They believe that the owl brings death. I believe this also, except in a metaphorical sense. I have experienced the deaths of many beliefs and reaction patterns that no longer serve my growth. For example, I have released the pattern of stuffing my feelings and avoiding conflict. I understand the healing power of emotion and am able to be present with my feelings and those of others. The wisdom of the owl has taught me to walk through my fears and to accept transformation on a daily basis.

My childhood dreams led me to believe that I had an important mission to accomplish. I knew I did not want to be a missionary, but I had few women role models. When we received an old copy of the *Saturday Evening Post* covering the coronation of Queen Elizabeth II, I knew I had found my childhood ideal. I thumb tacked her pictures on my bedroom walls. Mom made me a crown out of purple and gold wrapping paper. I was in heaven — I was a queen! This experience reminds me of the nobility and purity of a child's dreams and symbolizes my mother's love.

One of my most dramatic lessons came from an experience with an exotic snake. My parents and I traveled to one of the outlying villages and spent the night in a small hut. The next morning I was sitting on a camp stool reading, while my parents finished drinking their coffee. I looked up to see a small black snake moving in an undulating fashion. I was transfixed as I watched it dancing toward me. Dad yelled something to the native man who had accompanied us as our cook and servant. He quickly grabbed a heavy stick and clubbed the snake to death.

I cried as I watched the snake's mutilated body writhe in agony. It did not deserve to die. We were intruding upon its territory. Although I can understand my parents' concern for my safety, it would have been much simpler to move out of the snake's path and allow it to live. Instead, the attitude of the missionaries was to destroy whatever was in the way. It was a very strange religion that pitted God against man and man against nature. I was deeply saddened by the lack of tolerance and the separation from nature that surrounded me.

Unfortunately, I learned nothing about sexuality as a child other than the subliminal message that it was a forbidden subject. The unashamed nakedness of the native people was a sharp contrast to the guilt-ridden attitude of the white missionaries toward the human body. As a child I was confused by the dichotomy of cultures. Nevertheless, I focused on being a good little girl so that my parents and God would approve of me.

The only childhood exploration of my body occurred as a sleep inducer. Tucked into my mosquito-netted bed, I would often stroke my stomach lightly with my fingertips, drifting off to sleep on the delicious waves of pleasure created by this touch. I sometimes extended the stroking to my arms and as yet undeveloped breasts. I only caressed my upper body. Never did it occur to me to touch my genitals. They were for utilitarian purposes of elimination only. It would be years before I awoke to the mysterious pleasures awaiting my discovery. First, I would experience the path of abuse.

My innocence and trust were mirrored by an incident involving Kanangila, a young native man who worked as one of our servants. He desperately wanted to own a gramophone so that he could make music. He had seen one in the market and would occasionally return just to look at the gramophone while dreaming of being the star of his village with his magical box. For a year Kanangila saved his money. He buried his coins underneath his hut for safekeeping. He could not bury paper money because the white ants would have eaten it. Finally the day arrived that Kanangila had enough coins to make his purchase. He began his three-hour trek early in the morning, walking as fast as he could. At the market he carefully counted out all of his coins and hugged the gramophone to him as he began his journey home. Overcome by excitement, he stopped in the jungle to play his magic box. He wound the crank as he had seen the merchant do and waited for the music to begin. Nothing happened. He wound it some more. Again, nothing happened. He wound and wound the crank until it broke off, and still there was no music. Completely frustrated, he shook the box, and waited again. Then he threw it on the ground and jumped up and down on it, smashing the gramophone. Kanangila

29

had spent his life savings, and in his trusting innocence, he had expected to be able to make music. He had not been told that he needed to have a record in order to play his magic box.

My sexuality was like Kanangila's experience with the gramophone. I was never given any information. Like Kanangila, my innocence and lack of understanding would lead to extreme frustration and disappointment. Most of us were equally ill prepared to deal with our sexuality. What little information we did receive as children was negative programming. It was the silence surrounding the subject of sexuality that conditioned us to feel shame, guilt, and fear.

My strict religious programming did not prepare me for the pressures placed on young girls in the United States. Innocent and trusting, I did not know how to protect myself sexually since I did not know where babies came from. I had been taught that men were superior to women and that they needed to be pleased no matter what the sacrifice to me. Although my parents gave me the upbringing they believed was appropriate for a young Christian girl, they created a sexual time bomb, ready to explode into womanhood without the protection of information and understanding of sexuality.

Δ Δ Δ

When I was ten years old, we began preparing to leave Africa. We would visit family in Europe and then travel by ocean liner to the United States. My parents planned to apply for citizenship. I felt that they were abandoning their Dutch heritage, but even more, I felt heartbroken about leaving my Africa.

Shortly before our departure I had an experience in ecstasy and oneness that has profoundly influenced my journey. Schoolwork completed for the day and book of mythology under my arm, I skipped toward my favorite hideout. It was a short distance to the giant mango tree, overlooking a lemon and orange grove behind our house. I reached the tree, spread out my quilt, and snacked on a succulent mango, wiping the drops of juicy sweetness from my hands onto the grass. My fingers were still sticky, so I licked them before I lay down to experience the beauty of my surroundings.

The shocking blueness of the tropical sky was softened by a family of cumulus clouds, towering majestically over the hillside. These ephemeral reminders of spirit guardians were scurrying to their appointment with the thunderstorm that promised its welcome refreshment with distant rumbles. The richness of the dense foliage, wildflowers, and graceful palm trees melted into the vastness of the sky and the clouds. It was a sky that remembered how to be blue, a sky to get lost in. Far above, a hawk circled slowly.

Looking up through the canopy of leaves on the mango tree, I slipped into an altered state of consciousness. I felt a deep sense of oneness with the sky, the Earth, and the untamed nature that surrounded me. In my imagination I began to ride on one of the thunderclouds, pausing briefly to view the rainstorm and to dance in the clouds beneath my feet. I hugged the raindrops and tasted their cool wetness. My imagination led me to travel faster and faster, as though I were flying, the land below me blending into a rich kaleidoscope of green, brown, and gold. I began floating effortlessly into the magical kaleidoscope that was my beloved Africa. I felt my love for the Earth and all of her creatures, experiencing a deep sense of calm and oneness with the universe.

I did not know then that I had experienced ecstasy and that the memory of that moment would remain with me for a lifetime. When I became aware of my surroundings, I jumped up and hugged my friend, the mango tree.

Δ Δ Δ

Our life in Africa was hard. It was a time of sacrifice and service. There were few luxuries, and we learned to live with few material possessions. Yet I consider myself fortunate to have grown up in Central Africa. It was a rewarding experience that taught me many lessons.

I felt a haunting sadness associated with our departure. I was ten years old and wanted to remain young and innocent forever. Not knowing if we would ever return, I sadly packed my most precious possessions in a small trunk and said a tearful farewell to my African home. It was time for my journey to America, the Promised Land!

Chapter 5

Rape of Innocence

"Land! They've sighted land!" My brother's excited cry made my heart beat rapidly with anticipation. A short while later a tugboat arrived to guide our ocean liner into the harbor. As we drew closer to New York City, I watched the sun shining brightly on the Statue of Liberty. She seemed to be stretching her arms in welcome toward our ship and especially toward me. I jumped up and down with excitement. We were finally coming to the land and the life I had read about and dreamed of for years. As we disembarked, everywhere I looked were man-made wonders and luxuries that made life in the jungle seem primitive.

What followed were experiences in culture shock that served to educate me into the American way of life. At age ten I was abruptly introduced to such marvels as four-lane highways, sky scrapers, radios that worked, television with multichannel violence, commercials that made boastful promises, department stores with sales clerks with painted doll faces and high heels, and ladies in fur coats. I was enchanted by the supermarkets with their rows and rows of tempting "foreign" foods including white bread that I buttered and squashed into dough balls and rolled in white sugar. Mom's home-made bread had never been that soft! Every day was an adventure wrapped in plastic and aluminum foil with neon lights that flashed, "Explore me if you dare. This is America, the land of opportunity and opportunists."

We moved often. First, to Florida for a few months, to Tennessee for a year, and then to Indiana. Although I missed the quiet simplicity of life in the African jungle, my quest for understanding and knowledge about my new home country was uppermost in my mind. I wanted to be an American — I wanted desperately to fit in.

My first day of American public school was an experiment in terror. Because of my home schooling, I was two years ahead of my age group. I felt as though everyone were staring at me when my parents and I walked into the school building to register me for the sixth grade. Even though I was younger than anyone in my class, I was the tallest and the skinniest. I felt awkward and different from everyone else in my green plaid dress and new saddle oxfords. My first year of American public education introduced me to senseless rules, oversized classes, busy-work, standardized testing, tasteless cafeteria food, and social cliques. I was fortunate to have an enlightened teacher who urged me to cherish my culturally rich background. She also encouraged my love of writing.

It was during the sixth grade that I began noticing that boys were cute. My first boyfriend was Jerry. Since we had no car, Mom would walk me to school and return to walk me home every afternoon. One day she was late, and instead of waiting for her, I walked to my house with Jerry. He returned my interest by kicking me in the shins. I still liked him and assumed that boys did things like that to girls.

Until I was fourteen, boys did not seem to like me. They used to make fun of my skinny body and hairy legs, but they made no advances. We lived in a military town, and the servicemen I met at church looked handsome in their uniforms. Whenever one of them would be nice to me, I would fall in love. Then he would ignore me, and my heart would be broken for days.

Although my sexuality was budding, I still was not certain where babies came from. I suspected it started with passionate kissing. Mom had given me a Christian girl's guidebook, assuming that it would give me all the information I needed. I read with fascination the story of Susie, who went to the movies with her boyfriend and started kissing and petting on the back row. The book said that what followed was a horrible sin. It did not say what the sin was or how it happened. It skipped to the fact that Susie got pregnant and drank a bottle of lye which almost killed her. She had to have her stomach pumped, and that was the end of the book. I was too shy to question my mother about what I had read. The images of sin and stomach pumps were too much for me to want to know more. I focused on school and church and on being good.

The onset of my menstrual cycle when I was twelve was a traumatic experience, which reinforced my feelings of shame about my body. I was getting ready for school one morning when I noticed a pinkish-red stain on my panties. I was horrified! Images of bleeding to death darted through my mind. Then I remembered having once seen my mother place a blood-stained pad in the bathroom trash when we were in Africa. I had started to cry, fearful that she was hurt or had a terrible disease. "Oh, that's just from my *gedoetje,*" she had stated with no further explanation.

What exactly was a *gedoetje,* and had I caught it? I found my mother in the kitchen, washing the breakfast dishes. I told her that I was sick and bleeding. She did not act alarmed, just embarrassed. Mom told me that I could stay home from school and that she would go to the store to purchase a box of tampons for me. She said that she had always had to use sanitary pads, which were messy and smelly. She added that perhaps I would be able to suffer through the discomfort and inconvenience of my *gedoetje* each month with a more modern approach. She did not tell me how to use the tampons. I had to figure that out by myself.

I locked myself in the bathroom, opened the box, and read the instruction leaflet. Then I placed one leg on the edge of the bathtub, as directed, and tried to insert a tampon into my vagina. It was dry and it hurt to try to force the cardboard applicator. I was unsure if I was even aiming at the right spot. I had to use a hand mirror to find the opening. It took at least half a dozen tampons before I was able to insert one properly. It felt painful, awkward, and embarrassing to have to touch myself down there. I worried that I might walk funny with the tampon inside me. I went back to bed that morning, feeling embarrassed, abandoned, and confused. There was no one to comfort me or assure me that I was okay.

Entering womanhood should be a celebration. Instead I received the message that being a woman was going to be painful and awkward. Indigenous societies celebrate the onset of a young girl's moon cycle as a time of rejoicing and welcoming her into womanhood. A woman is considered to be her most powerful during her moon cycle. It is a travesty that our culture has labeled this "the curse."

In one of my workshops a young Afro-American woman, named Janet, described her experience of her first menstrual period. She also had no information on what to expect, but she instinctively knew that it was a special occasion. She announced to her family that she would do no chores that day and wanted to be left alone. She created her own ceremony in her room with candles and music, dancing to honor her new experience. What a healthy way to welcome womanhood!

My mother, who is eighty-nine, recently revealed an incident that explained why it was impossible for her to talk to me about menstruation. When she was in mission training in London, she had a traumatic experience during her moon cycle. It was a Sunday. She had spent the day witnessing door-to-door, inviting people to a service that evening. By the time she was ready to return to her dormitory, she was cramping and bleeding heavily. She almost fainted as she rode her bicycle through London traffic. Mom knew she was too weak to go to the evening service. She went to see the director, a woman who had spent many years as a missionary in China. The director spoke patronizingly to my mother, who was thirty-one years old at that time. "What is wrong, child?"

Mom collapsed onto a chair and requested permission to go to bed because it was the bad time of the month for her. The director's harsh demeanor turned to ice. She pointed a bony finger at my mother as she stated, "Do not ever again dare to mention such a forbidden subject to anyone again — ever! Now, go change your clothes. Hurry up, or you will be late for the service."

This story has given me understanding of my mother's programming of shame, guilt, and fear. It has helped me to forgive her for not preparing me for womanhood.

An incident in my ninth grade history class aroused my curiosity. The teacher had left the room for a coffee break, while we supposedly worked on a homework assignment. One of the boys near the front of the room started passing a condom wrapped in a sheet of notebook paper around to the girls. Each of them would unfold the paper and then squeal in mock horror. When it came time to show me the paper, he skipped me with the reasoning, "You aren't supposed to know about this. You're a preacher's daughter." Everyone laughed, and I still did not know what was in the paper.

My first experience with masturbation was an accidental discovery at age fourteen that inserting a tampon was pleasurable. I got up in the middle of the night to go to the bathroom and change my tampon. As I slid the replacement easily into my vagina, a tingle of pleasurable sensations spread through my genitals. I was startled by what I had felt. I removed the tampon and reinserted the applicator, arching my back as I slid the tube in and out of my vagina. I did not know what I was doing, but I felt ashamed that I liked it so much. Even though I still did not know about sexual intercourse, I knew it must be sinful to touch myself down there. I was too heavily programmed with fear to masturbate again until many years later.

The only occasion which suggested that my parents engaged in sexual intercourse occurred a few weeks later. I was awakened in the middle of the night by their bedroom light shining into my room across the hall. I heard them talking and moving around and decided to investigate. I stood in their doorway, watching in disbelief, as they changed the sheets on their bed. They were fully clothed, Dad in faded blue pajamas and Mom in her long, flannel nightgown.

"Is something wrong?" I asked. "Are you sick?"

They acted embarrassed, trying to pretend that changing sheets at two o'clock in the morning was not unusual. The next morning I asked Mom about it. She seemed annoyed and said that nothing was wrong. I wondered why she insisted on changing sheets at such an odd hour. Probably some semen dribbled onto the sheets after their lovemaking. My mother, who prides herself on being a good Dutch housewife, must have considered that the semen made the sheets dirty. She could never stand anything dirty, especially anything to do with body fluids.

I can remember asking Mom one more time where babies came from. She repeated, "When a man and a woman live together as husband and wife." Then she abruptly left the room, abandoning me to find out about sex without guidance or protection, and most of all, without love.

Shortly before my fifteenth birthday we went to Florida for our summer vacation. All I could see was scantily dressed young men with muscles and dark tans. Going for a walk along the beach with my parents was like trolling. My body had developed, and I had received an electric razor for Christmas to rid my legs of their hairy fuzz. Boys no longer ridiculed me. Instead, they stared. I had a slender figure, long legs, and long, golden blonde hair. My parents were justifiably nervous. I was boy crazy, but I did not know why. I was innocent and I was eager.

I met Tex on one of these trolling expeditions. He was right in our path, holding out a frisbee to me. "Want to play?" he asked.

My parents were ready to return to our cottage across the highway from the beach. I pleaded with them to let me stay and play. They reluctantly agreed. After I played frisbee with Tex, he invited me to go to the movies. It took a great deal of pleading with my parents before I received permission to go on my first real date. I was supposed to wait until I was sixteen to date officially. They did not even know this nineteen-year-old Texan with his shy smile and eager eyes, yet they let me go. I was proud of them for being so liberal — so American.

Sexy, horny, and completely uninformed about sexuality, I had my first date. It was a date that would scar my life for many years. After the movies we walked along the beach. Before I realized what was happening, Tex had pushed me down behind a sand dune and was all over me. I tried to push him away, but he had me pinned down. He pulled down my shorts and panties, and I felt something hard and painful enter me. After a few quick pumps, he shuddered and rolled off me. At first I was not sure what had happened, but Tex no longer seemed to be a physical threat. I felt frightened, sad, and confused.

As we walked home, I complained about the messy wetness running down my leg and ran to the water's edge to wash it off. Tex laughed, "Haven't you ever had that on you before?" I did not answer. I was ready to go home.

I was too scared afterward to tell my parents, and I never considered the possibility of reporting Tex to the police for rape. I lay awake that night thinking of the bottle of lye and the stomach pump. I cried myself to sleep because of my unexplainable feelings of loss, guilt, and shame. I was afraid that I might go to hell because of what had happened. The next morning I asked Mom, "How does a woman know when she is not pregnant?"

"When her *gedoetje* starts," was my mother's answer.

During the next week I could think of little other than what would happen if I were pregnant. I waited and worried myself into a high fever. My parents immediately went into the nurturing mode of my childhood. They pampered me and prayed over me. They called a doctor, who prescribed antibiotics, a rather unusual treatment for the trauma of rape. One nervous week later my period started, and I knew I had been protected by my guardian angel.

That was my sex education. I still did not fully understand, and I was not knowledgeable enough to realize that I had been raped. I knew something terribly sinful had happened and assumed I was to blame. I felt that I must be a bad person, a very evil person. It was many years before I recognized and healed the psychological trauma of this abuse. My compliant, enabling behavior and my lack of information had set the trap for a traumatic first sexual intercourse experience. It has taken years for me to release my anger toward a religion that programmed me to believe that my body was evil and that sex was a shameful act. Because of their religion, my parents did not prepare me for my initiation into the sacrament of sexuality. They abandoned me when I most needed honest information and understanding. Instead of having a beautiful memory, I was violated. I consider this a form of religious, as well as sexual abuse.

I have been able to forgive Tex for his heartless act of rape. He was the product of his religious and societal programming, the product of a sick culture that breeds domination and abuse of women. I have found it much more difficult to forgive the religion that positioned me for this trauma and abuse. My circumstances were unusual. It is difficult to imagine anyone being so naive. With the explicitness of television, movies, and books, today's youth are usually knowledgeable about the basics of sex. Yet the attitude of guilt and shame, the attitude of denial typical of patriarchal religions still causes serious emotional trauma for many young women and men. Those who are not raped physically may have equally ugly scars of emotional and psychological abuse. When abuse occurs, the typical reaction is to shut down the emotions and bury the incident in years of denial.

Denial is not the answer for dealing with our woundedness. It has taken courage and perseverance to undertake my journey of Sacred Sexuality. A combination of bodywork and breathwork has helped me to release my rage and emotional pain. I have used methods from Neuro-Linguistic Programming to reimprint my brain so that the past no longer haunts me.

We can transform our woundedness into our greatest strength. Abuse, abandonment, and the resulting pain can be our sacred teachers. They shake us to the core of our being, strengthening our resolve to undertake the sacred journey into our soul. We will experience healing when we accept the lesson in every painful event.

41

Many of us have been abused — psychologically, physically, and sexually. Some people find it difficult to understand that woundedness can be a sacred teacher. They remain stuck in anger and pain. Many others use the experience of their abuse as a catalyst for growth. In coming to terms with my abuse, I acknowledge its lessons: understanding, forgiveness, compassion, self-empowerment, courage, and a call to action. It is through facing our woundedness and understanding its gifts that we can free ourselves to embrace our journey of Sacred Sexuality.

Chapter 6

Taking the Predictable Path to Sex

Being raped did not make me afraid of men. Instead, I went into denial about the whole experience, pretending that it had never happened. I returned to school and all evidences of a normal life. My parents allowed me to begin dating when I was fifteen, the youngest junior in my Indiana high school.

The first boy I fell for was the president of the senior class. Darrell's 6'4" height, assured good looks, and popularity made me feel giddy when he stopped by my locker to flirt. We dated occasionally, mostly as a convenience to him. He told me I was the kind of girl that guys marry. Once, Darrell abandoned me shortly after we arrived at a dance so that he could park with his fast girlfriend who would go all the way. I allowed Darrell to use me just to have the opportunity to go out on dates. I spent hours in my room listening to sad songs on the radio and crying. I felt unlovable and unworthy.

My peers treated me like an outsider because I was a preacher's daughter. I was considered a nice girl who did not go beyond kissing. When my church youth group went camping, the excitement of the weekend was a well-read and dog-eared copy of *Peyton Place,* a sexually explicit novel. Although the girl who brought the book was rather homely, the boys surrounded her constantly. I felt sad and left out.

By my senior year I had started going out with Joe, which meant I had started parking with Joe. We seldom drove farther than a deserted road where we would park and kiss for hours at a time. One evening we sneaked into the basement of our church, which was next door to my house. Joe and I lay down on the ping-pong table. His body pressing against mine felt exciting and sinful. We kept our clothes on while we kissed and squirmed on the hard green table. Joe shuddered for a few seconds as he accidentally ejaculated in his jeans. We did not discuss what had happened, but he acted embarrassed. I felt guilty and ashamed. Three weeks passed before Joe called me again. While I waited, I listened to sad songs on the radio and agonized over having lost his affection. When Joe called, we went parking again, although we did not repeat our experience with the ping-pong table.

I never considered having intercourse before marriage. In my mind I was still a virgin. Joe was Catholic and not someone my parents approved of or considered worthy of me. Prejudice was strong in my family, and my parents urged me to date someone of our religion. They explained that even though I was too young to get married, the purpose of dating was to find a suitable husband. A suitable husband should be of my religious faith so that we would not be "unequally yoked together." He was also supposed to be stronger than me spiritually because he would be the spiritual head of our household, responsible to God for me. I was indoctrinated with these patriarchal beliefs during my teenage years and did not question the authority that my future husband would have over my spiritual well-being. I accepted the dogma which taught that because I was a woman, I needed a man in order to have validity in society and in heaven.

I met Jack at a Christian youth rally. He was 6'2" tall, with dark, wavy hair and blue eyes. When I stood to be introduced as one of the speakers, he whispered to a friend, "Well, you can always dream!" He fell in love with me instantly. Jack had grown up in Mississippi and had a classic Southern grace and charm. After the meeting my parents were planning to drive the sixty miles back home rather than stay for dinner. Some of my friends from church were staying and offered me a ride home. Mom and Dad were so protective that I had to plead with them to let me stay. I was a senior in high school, and they still treated me like a child.

Arriving in the dining area late, I could not find a place to sit with my girlfriends. The only seat available was next to Jack. He was eating carrot and celery sticks when he began flirting with me. His attention made me feel special. A week later I received a letter from him saying that he would be attending another youth rally in a different city. He expressed an interest in seeing me there. I convinced my mother to go with me to the meeting. Jack and I did not attend the afternoon rally. Instead he drove me to a lakeside park. It was springtime in Indiana, and we parked in a secluded spot near the lake, where he introduced me to French kissing and fondling. His kissing drew me into a spiral of delightful sensations. I felt as though I were awakening from a deep sleep, like a beautiful rosebud opening in the warmth of the springtime sun. When he shyly caressed my breasts through my blouse, he stirred my desire for physical and spiritual union.

When my mother met Jack, she approved of him and did not even seem to mind that I had skipped the meeting. She and Dad agreed that I could invite Jack to spend the weekend with us, which he did, two weeks later. Then he invited me to his graduation dance, and I spent the weekend at his parents' house. By that time I was convinced that he was the man of my dreams. I was in love, real love, for the first time in my young life. We talked about marriage and about having four children. He proposed to me a few weeks later as we sat on the wooden swing on my front porch — I accepted. I was sixteen, a young high school graduate, and convinced that I knew what I wanted in a relationship that was to last forever.

When Jack asked me to wear his high school ring until he could afford an engagement ring, I proudly agreed. Having my first steady boyfriend made me feel that I had someone of my own who would never abandon me — ever. I finally felt as though I belonged. We used to sign our letters to each other, "love forever." I would never have to feel lonely again.

We quickly moved into heavier petting sessions, as Jack began to stroke my body into a frenzy of desire. I kept my clothes on but did not resist his pressure to let him touch me. Since we were going to be married, I rationalized that I was not being very sinful. One night, Jack broke the zipper on my brand new pair of dress slacks as he tried to touch my genitals. As he struggled to open the zipper, it resisted and then broke. I wondered if God were trying to keep me pure. I was horrified that Mom would discover my sin. The next morning I had to tell her that the expensive slacks we had bought had come apart. She must have thought that I was still naive about sex, because she did not question me about how it had happened. When I took the slacks back to the dress shop to be repaired, I felt as though all the saleswomen were staring at me knowingly. I was certain they could tell I had been behaving sinfully.

A few weeks later Mom walked in on Jack and me in front of the television in the darkened living room. We were lying on the couch, spoon fashion, holding each other. Her comment the next morning was laced with anger. "I don't ever want to see you lying like that with Jack again!"

"What do you mean, Mom?"

"You know... you were... against his parts. Nice girls don't do that!"

I understood that I was not being good any longer. I stuffed my guilt feelings and decided to have fun instead of being a nice girl.

Even though my parents were concerned about how quickly I had fallen in love, they were charmed by Jack. He had the ability to get his way with his sparkling blue eyes and quick smile. My parents were thrilled that Jack's family was of the same religious affiliation as ours. They also approved of his Southern upbringing. There seemed to be nothing in the way of our having a perfect courtship, ending of course, in the perfect marriage.

Jack and I went out of state to the University of Southern Mississippi together. My parents would have preferred that I stay home and go to the local junior college, but Jack and I were inseparable.

Rather than staying in a dormitory, Jack lived with his grandmother near campus. One day he had a cold and stayed home from classes. I played nurse while his grandmother was gone. I brought him a large glass of juice and leaned over to kiss him. He responded by throwing back the covers, exposing his nakedness. It was my first glimpse of an erection. I was scared and excited. Was Jack going to try to pressure me into having premarital sex?

I touched his penis hesitantly. He encouraged me to stroke it. I felt shy and nervous fondling him. He wanted me to get undressed and play together naked, but I refused. My mind was reeling with images of hell as a just punishment for girls who were not nice.

It was difficult for me to tell Jack about being raped on the beach. He was stunned but recovered well. He pretended that the incident had never occurred. His religious programming, like mine, provided a convenient way to handle emotions — you deny them.

My first major in college was music. I was almost kicked out of the music program when Jack and I were caught by a music professor in a passionate embrace in a darkened practice room. Because there was never enough time to practice the piano and the flute, I eventually changed my major to English. My parents and his convinced me to get a minor in education so that I could teach school if I ever needed a job to fall back on. That was what girls were supposed to do. My education was not for a career but simply a finishing school and an insurance policy for unforeseen disasters. There was never any expectation that I would be anything other than a wife and mother. That was the predictable path for young women at that time.

After two full years of college, including summer classes, I had accumulated enough credit hours to be classified as a senior. I had a passion for learning that had been instilled in me by my parents. It was predictable that my grades were much higher than Jack's. That was expected of girls.

I was eighteen when I became the June bride of my beloved Southern gentleman. Our wedding was on a Saturday afternoon. My father performed the traditional wedding service, with the vows of love, honor, and obey. We drove from Mississippi to New Orleans for our honeymoon. I waited nervously in our borrowed car while Jack checked us into a hotel in the French Quarter. We each grabbed a suitcase out of the car and walked toward room 212. He fumbled with the key and started to hold the door open for me. He quickly put his suitcase down and let the door slam in my face. "I have to carry you over the threshold," he insisted. Jack unlocked the door again, propping it open with his foot, and picked me up. He dropped me awkwardly on the bed, pulled off my shoes, and tried to undress me. I stopped him with a passionate kiss and told him he would have to wait while I unpacked my negligee. Locked in the bathroom, I took fifteen minutes to spread perfumed oil on my body, brush my hair, and put on my white gown and robe. I felt as though I were acting in a movie about two people sharing their wedding night. Everything had to be perfect. I moved slowly in excited anticipation, not wanting this moment to be over. I had waited so long for this — legal sex.

When Jack knocked on the door for the third time, I opened it and floated out of the bathroom. He pulled back the bedspread and took off his robe. I would like to say that we made passionate love all night long. That was how I had dreamed it would be. Instead, we grabbed each other, tumbled into bed, and with very little foreplay, Jack guided his erect penis into my vagina. He was young and inexperienced as a lover and anxious to please his new bride. He bounced up and down a few times and then ejaculated. It was over far too quickly for all my expectations of a wedding night. He held me tenderly for a few moments and then went to sleep. Since I knew so little about sex, I assumed that what we had shared was normal. I felt satisfied that at last I was really a woman. I had a husband and would now have a respectable place in society.

The next morning we attended church together, another predictable action for a minister's daughter. I wanted to start our marriage by honoring God. During our honeymoon we explored the French Quarter, holding hands as we visited shops and took a horse-and-buggy tour. We went to dinner and danced between courses of our expensive meal. Our lovemaking improved with each session, culminating in a long evening of foreplay during which we took a bath together. Jack dried me off, spread fragrant lotion on my damp body, and carried me into the bedroom. He kissed me passionately and caressed my breasts while I fondled his penis. He kissed and sucked my breasts as he entered me, moving more slowly and deliberately. When he ejaculated, I felt complete, even though I had not experienced an orgasm. I was happy to be married to Jack. He was a wonderful husband and a tender lover. I knew we would live happily ever after. A few days later we returned to college. I began playing house in earnest and dreamed of having a baby.

Our sex life was nice, although not as passionate as our courtship. We soon settled into a predictable life, with married friends, casserole dinners, and insurance premiums. There were times when I wondered if I were missing something by being married so young, but I quickly buried my thoughts.

One of my dreams was to attend graduate school. Instead, I got pregnant the only time we did not bother to use the diaphragm. We had no afternoon classes that rainy January day. We shared a light lunch together and began kissing between bites of peanut butter sandwiches. The thunder sounded ominous as Jack led me to the bedroom and undressed me. I had stopped taking birth control pills because of my concern about possible side effects. Once our passion intensified, neither of us wanted to stop long enough for me to insert my diaphragm. We made love accompanied by the sound of rain pelting against the bedroom window with thunder and lightning for special effects. When Jack ejaculated, I knew that I had conceived. It was not supposed to have happened yet. I had wanted to get an advanced degree. Nevertheless, I was thrilled — and scared.

Jack hoped that we would have a boy so that they could play ball together. I wished for a daughter to love and nurture, and I got my wish. Jackie was born six weeks after I graduated from college. When I held her in my arms, I realized that my dream had become a reality.

When we were dating, Jack had a born-again experience because of my insistent witnessing and sharing of Bible verses. He would have done anything to please me. He decided to study for the ministry, which thrilled my parents and me. We made plans to move to Chicago after graduation so that he could attend an evangelical seminary. With the financial assistance of both sets of parents, we made our big move, and Jack started seminary. One semester of Greek, Hebrew, and theology convinced him that he was not destined to be a minister. We left Chicago and moved in with my parents, making plans for Jack to enter graduate school.

The year after Jackie was born, I began teaching high school so that Jack could get his graduate degree. It was already time to fall back on my education. I worked hard at my job and my marriage. I had the perfect husband and a daughter whom I adored. Soon Jack would get the perfect job, and I could quit teaching and settle down to being a housewife and mother.

Our parents doted on their first grandchild. Jack's parents treated me like the daughter they had always wanted, buying me expensive clothing and taking us on a European vacation. Life was good, predictably so. Jack obtained a teaching position at a small junior college when he completed graduate school. We bought a home, an American car, a poodle, and were charged to the limit on our Visa card. Jack became a deacon in a conservative Presbyterian church, and I played the organ. We voted Republican and were the predictable couple in every way.

When our daughter was seven, she asked me, "Where do babies come from, Mama?" I told her that she was too young to discuss it. I was not comfortable talking about sex and began repeating my mother's pattern of avoidance. I remember her question as not being cute but embarrassing, predictably so.

We had been married for several years before we attempted oral sex. Deep programming left me feeling guilty when we experimented with sex in a way that seemed sinful and unclean. Our lovemaking had become routine. I remember only rare moments when we were passionate in our sex life.

On one occasion we made love three times in one day. Jack had just returned from a three-week trip to Europe, and I stayed home from work to be with him. I craved having an exciting love life together, but the romance did not last. We would have sex every two or three weeks, and that seemed to satisfy him. When we did make love, I felt as though I was playing the role of seductress. I would dress in a sheer negligee, light candles in our bedroom, and try to woo this man who was my husband into becoming the lover of my dreams. He was intimidated by my high expectations for our love life. He would try to please me, but after a few minutes of pumping, he would ejaculate, leaving me unfulfilled and fantasizing about God-man. I yearned for a sexual partner with whom I could share a deep spiritual communion. This mythical figure took the shape of God-man, a man who was powerful and tender, spiritual and sexy, and who would drive me wild in bed.

So I began to flirt with strangers. It was safe and provided a rush of adrenalin. I never considered the possibility of being unfaithful to Jack. I loved him. He was a gentle person, although strongly opinionated. Our marriage began to stagnate because we did not communicate our needs and because we projected our romantic expectations of perfection onto each other. Whenever there was a conflict, we ignored it. Denial and passionless living became the norm.

We also grew apart because I was entering a period of quantum spiritual growth, while Jack was satisfied with staying exactly where he was. Jack and I used to love to drink coffee and talk. One day I stated that I would rather live half a life fully, than a full life halfway. Jack shook his head in disbelief. "You've got to be kidding! I would much rather live a full life halfway." I was reading philosophy and metaphysics and expanding my beliefs daily. He proudly stated that he had his belief system all worked out for the rest of his life and did not intend to change. That was the beginning of the end for us. The pain of disappointed hopes and dreams overwhelmed me as I began to consider the possibility that I would have to leave my marriage in order to keep from losing my soul on the predictable path. Our relationship was supposed to be perfect. It was supposed to fulfill all my desires and last forever. I felt lonely, sad, and disappointed.

By taking the predictable path, I lost myself in my roles of wife, mother, teacher, and good Christian woman. In the process of conforming to the expectations of my family and society, I lost contact with my own identity and with my soul. The predictable path is one chosen by millions of women and men who are searching for love, joy, and fulfillment. The fallacy of trying to find fulfillment in a committed relationship is that the answers to our happiness are never found in someone else. The typical experience of romantic love is the projection of our ideals of perfection onto our less than perfect partner. A relationship built on false expectations is certain to cause frustration and disappointment.

It is possible to have a partnership that is healthy and promotes individual expression and growth of the partners. Being in a committed relationship with someone who is also on a path of growth is a dance of joy.

Chapter 7

Who Are You?

The yoga class was already in session when I arrived. The instructor, Carolyn, was completing her preview of the postures we would be covering that evening. I had barely seated myself in the lotus position when she singled me out from the group with the question, "Who are you?"

"I'm Marina and I'm late!"

"We know that. Who are you?"

Her response took me by surprise, and I stammered, "Uh ... Who am I? Well ... I'm a mother."

"Who are you?" Carolyn repeated.

"This is some kind of a game, right?"

Carolyn did not smile and repeated, "Who are you?"

"I'm a wife."

Her questioning was relentless. "Who are you?"

"I'm a teacher."

"Who are you?"

I thought I understood what Carolyn wanted, but she did not seem satisfied with my answers. "I'm a daughter."

"Who are you?"

"I'm a Christian."

"Who are you?"

"I am a musician."

"Who are you?"

"I am a naturalized citizen of the United States."

"Who are you?"

Suddenly I had run out of roles. I stammered, "Uh ... I wish I knew what you were looking for, Carolyn."

"Who are you?"

She was not going to stop. The entire class was waiting for me to get the right answer. Some were smiling as though they knew the answer, while others looked as puzzled as I. Who else could I be besides all the roles I had mentioned? I closed my eyes and breathed deeply. Then I opened my mouth to speak, unsure of what I would say. I just knew I had to say something. "I ... I am ..."

"That's better." Carolyn smiled. "Now, who are you?"

"But I didn't finish. I just said, 'I am.'"

"That's a wonderful beginning. Who are you?"

I was perspiring in my leotard. This could go on all night. "Okay, I am ... I am ..." and then I got it! "I am an individual. I am me!" It felt as though a river of understanding was breaking loose from my soul which had been frozen in conformity. "I'm a free spirit. I am love. I am searching. I am hungry for understanding. I am alone. I am scared. I am ready for more. I am unlimited. I am ... I am ... I am ... I am here for a purpose. I am on a mission. I'm excited!"

"Yes, Marina, you are all those things and more. Keep searching and you will begin to awaken from your sleep. When we stop identifying with all of our roles, we open ourselves to remembering who we really are. Those who spend their lives believing that they are their job, their marriage, and all the personae they take on, will remain asleep. They will miss the greatest joy in life — the joy of remembering our true selves and our mission on the planet."

I was flushed with the excitement of my discovery. The rest of the evening went by quickly, and I rushed home. I could hardly wait to tell Jack about my understanding — remembering — of myself.

Jack had gone to bed early. I woke him up as I rushed into the darkened bedroom. "Are you awake, Honey? There's something I have to tell you."

"I'm awake now," he groaned. "Can't it wait till morning? I had just fallen asleep."

"Please don't be grumpy. I want to share with you how happy I am."

I switched on the light and sat down on the bed. Reaching for his hand, I tried to explain what I had discovered. "In yoga class tonight, Carolyn, the instructor, singled me out to ask the question, Who are you? At first I didn't get it right. I was stuck in all my roles, and then ..."

He was snoring. For a moment I felt the familiar fear of abandonment. Jack had abandoned me by not being interested enough to stay awake. I pushed the fear aside and focused on the simplicity and the beauty of what had happened in class. I knew I was more than all those predictable roles I had listed. Yet they were always in the forefront of my mind. I had been forced to see that I was much more than my roles. I looked at my present life as superficial, as merely a shell of what it could be.

I introspectively went through my nightly routine of removing my makeup, flossing and brushing my teeth, and putting on my nightgown. I slipped into bed, hugging my side of the king-size mattress. I wanted to fall asleep remembering more about who I was. I did not want to be near this man who had abandoned me by falling asleep.

I awoke with a deep sense of peace and joy. It no longer seemed important to share all my experiences with Jack. I looked at his sleeping form on the other side of the bed and no longer felt abandoned. I could never be abandoned as long as I remembered my true self. The yoga class experience supported my belief that I had a sacred mission and that I was embarking on an inner journey. I had received the call to myself and must follow my intuitive guidance. It was my responsibility to continue the journey, no matter what the costs. My destiny was not within the confines of the predictable path.

Δ Δ Δ

Each of us receives the call to begin the journey back to ourself. It is that moment of enlightenment in which we recognize that we are much more than who we thought we were. The veil between our conscious and unconscious selves is lifted, and for a moment we glimpse the eternity within our soul. The journey into the self leads us to abandon the security of the predictable life, charting our path into the high mountainous territory of our soul. The path is fraught with risk, danger, loneliness, and the promise of reconnecting with our innermost selves, our Inner Soulmate. It is through this journey back home that we begin living our destiny and open ourselves to ecstasy.

To undertake your journey back to yourself does not mean that you have to radically change your life by getting a divorce, changing careers, or changing lifestyles. It does require changing your inner dialogue, changing beliefs and reaction patterns, and changing the way you interact with others. How do you know when you are on your journey back to your Inner Soulmate? If you are uncertain, then you have not fully committed yourself to the journey. This journey cannot be made with partial commitment. Your awakening will leave no doubt.

Chapter 8

X-Rated Fantasies

Many women would have been thrilled to have a husband like Jack. He was kind, nurturing, and he loved me. He had been my cheerleader when I opened my business. He had agreed to take care of the household duties while I worked twelve-hour days, trying to balance my time between teaching school, running the business, and being a wife and mother. One of my friends had described Jack as just the right combination of scholarliness and virility for me. I was not sure about the virility part.

Although we did not discuss the fact that I was bored with our sex life, Jack was aware that my interest in sex was intensifying. When I told him that I wanted to go to an X-rated movie, he pretended resistance, but then agreed it might be fun. The first movie we attended was disgusting. It had no plot and showed scene after scene of women in various positions that exposed their buttocks and large breasts. The men's bodies were not fully exposed. I found the movie to be distasteful and exploitative of women.

The second movie was an X-rated documentary which

came to our attention when the local television news covered the story of a fundamentalist religious group picketing the theater. The night we attended there was a long line of people outside the theater, some wearing dark glasses and overcoats, hiding their faces from possible television cameras. There was no sign of the picketers or the news reporters. It felt titillating to be standing in that line. What if my parents found out? That thought made me even more excited about being naughty. I was discovering a latent rebelliousness in my attitude toward my sexual repression. I was ready to break free from the taboos of my fundamentalist programming. I was ready to discover uninhibited sexual passion.

The movie was hard-core pornography, thinly disguised as a documentary. I especially enjoyed the close-up shots of men's penises as they were given oral sex by their partners. I received more sex information than all my reading had provided. I caressed Jack's penis through his pants as I sat mesmerized in the darkened theater. I was ready to go home and orgasm together as the movie had shown.

When we got home, I lit candles and dressed in a sheer gown. Fantasizing that we were making an X-rated movie, I began kissing and sucking Jack's penis. When he was fully erect, I got on top of him and began moving slowly, sensuously, his penis penetrating my vagina. I was ready to make love all night, but the extra stimulation made Jack ejaculate long before I had begun to tap into the passion that lay hidden within me like an unopened book. All my excitement faded as I realized that our sex life would always be predictable and unfulfilling. Tears of frustration flowed down my cheeks as I contemplated my future with Jack. I had been married for thirteen years and had never had an orgasm. Feeling cheated and empty, I fell asleep, fantasizing about having a lover who would help me to awaken to my sexuality.

My sexual fantasies were beginning to preoccupy

me. Out of desperation, I bought a book on self-pleasuring and locked myself in the bathroom with a hand mirror and a flashlight, ready to explore my body. When I gently touched my clitoris, it responded with a subtle quiver. I touched it again and felt a shiver of delightful sensations move up my spine. I slowly placed my finger inside my vagina, following the step-by-step instructions on how to masturbate. Although the sensations were pleasurable, I felt frustrated because I was not sure what an orgasm would feel like. Unable to release into the feelings of pleasure, I became disgusted with trying to experience my body with a book for a partner. I had read articles on the big O and wondered if my capacity for pleasure measured up to the norm. I was wishing I could experience even a little O.

Jack was not responding to my heightened interest in sex. He even seemed threatened by my behavior. Whenever we did make love, I always checked my nipples afterward to see if they were hard. My book had said that hard nipples were an indication of having had an orgasm — mine were not hard.

Δ Δ Δ

In an attempt to add romance and excitement to my life, I began dreaming of traveling to Europe. I applied with a tour company to serve as chaperone for my high school French students and enrolled enough participants to receive a free trip for Jack and me. He refused to go. Our daughter, Jackie, had become a star softball player, and Jack did not want to miss any of her games. I argued with him that there would be many other games and that the trip would be like a second honeymoon. He would not budge, so I went to Europe without him.

I stuffed my feelings of abandonment. It was silly to feel resentful about his choice. Yet our relationship had changed since Jackie had begun to excel in softball. Jack, a frustrated athlete who had been forced to drop out of sports in high school because of injuries, was reliving his athletic dreams through our daughter. I felt that he was ignoring me, giving Jackie all his attention.

Europe did not disappoint me. I met a Frenchman named Jean-Pierre who was the Paris representative for the tour company. I felt attracted to him, not for his physical appearance, but for his energy and vitality. He was about forty, my height, with a wiry build. He was not particularly handsome — balding, with wire-rim glasses. I was attracted to his vibrancy and joie de vivre. He was sexy!

While my students unloaded luggage from the tour bus, I accepted Jean-Pierre's invitation to have a drink in a nearby cafe. He spoke French to me in a way that appealed to my craving for romance. He told me that my eyes were beautiful and that I must be very gifted. I did not know how to respond to such flattery. My hormones responded by lubricating my vagina.

That evening my students and I took a boat ride on the Seine River. The city of Paris glowed in the golden rays of the setting sun. I was flushed with the excitement of meeting Jean-Pierre and hoped to see him again. He was waiting at the dock when our boat returned. He invited me to have a drink with him after I accompanied my students back to the hotel.

I took a taxi to the Paris Hilton, where Jean-Pierre was waiting in the lounge area. The drink he ordered for me was called *L'Ambuscade,* which translates "The Ambush." I was unaccustomed to drinking strong liquor, and my drink and the romance of the moment made me feel light-headed. After our drink Jean-Pierre drove me to my hotel and kissed me good-night. I allowed myself to be drawn into a passionate embrace that would change my life. He did not ask to come up to my room. I doubt that I would have been able to resist.

The experience was overwhelming. I did not want to be unfaithful to Jack, but I did not know how to deal with my desires. That was my only experience in kissing another man during my marriage. It magnified my desire for passionate sex. From that point on I began to seriously fantasize what it would be like to go beyond kissing with a new lover. My early marriage seemed like a mistake as I regretted that I had not done more dating before getting married. I felt imprisoned by an unfulfilling marriage and by my strict religious programming that required me to spend a lifetime with a man whom I had chosen when I was sixteen. I knew that I could not remain a prisoner forever.

When I returned home, the differences between Jack and me were magnified. I considered his energy level lethargic compared to other men, especially the sexy Frenchmen. In the past we had walked at the same pace. Now I would walk to the end of the block and sit on the curb, waiting for this man who was becoming a stranger to me. Jack had experienced several mild occurrences of irregular heart palpitations called arrhythmia. He was paranoid of having a heart attack and had begun to move slowly through life.

Jack's philosophy was firmly in place, a rigid fundamentalist Christian philosophy. He had stopped growing, while I felt as though my life were just beginning. I knew that I had an important mission to fulfill although I did not know how to find it. I remembered Jack's statement that he would rather live a full life halfway and I cried. I cried for the loss of my dream of the perfect marriage. I cried for my awakening sexuality that could not find fulfillment. I cried for the sparkling eyes that no longer winked at me. I felt abandoned in my unhappiness.

My parents assumed that I was happy. They loved Jack and worshiped Jackie. It was impossible for me to talk to them. Marital problems were not discussed in my family. Denial and prayer were my programmed responses. I was expected to repress my emotions and be a good Christian woman.

Δ Δ Δ

Over half of all marriages end in divorce. Our society and our religion encourage us to believe that our marriage partner is our other half. When one of the halves is growing in the opposite direction from the other, conflict occurs which can destroy the relationship. Without skills in communication, trust breaks down between the partners, and they either choose to stay together in a shell of a marriage or they split apart.

It is time for a new model of relationship that is based on a sacred partnership between two whole, self-actualized individuals. The relationship that supports the individual growth of each partner is vibrant and alive. It encourages the maximizing of our physical, mental, emotional, and spiritual selves. It is a celebration of life and of love.

Chapter 9

Farewell to Innocence

Three years passed. I continued to harbor my secret longing for sexual fulfillment and for finding my life's purpose. In just three more years our daughter would graduate from high school, and I would feel justified in making my escape. There had been good times during the three previous years. I had tried to forget my fantasies and be a good Christian wife and mother. Then I experienced a Dreamtime that terrified me.

Jack and I had just gotten home from church. Every Sunday we would have a disagreement over the minister's sermon. That usually led to an argument about my business. On that particular Sunday, Jack was blaming my business for our differences. "I don't understand why you can't be like other women. Why don't you just close the business and go back to a normal job, like teaching school? You should never have let your teaching certificate expire. Now all your ambition has turned you into a cold-hearted bitch — a businesswoman!"

I stormed out of the den and into the bedroom, slamming the door. What nerve he had! Three more years, three more years, I kept repeating as I threw myself

64

onto the bed. Trying to relax, I did some deep breathing to release the anger that was making my stomach churn. Slowly relaxing, I drifted into an altered state of consciousness.

I was drawn into a tunnel of light, moving rapidly upward through the tunnel into a breathtaking mist of swirling rainbow light. Suddenly I began falling through the tunnel, falling faster and faster, downward, faster and faster. I saw an image in my free fall that haunted me for years. I looked in a mirror as I fell, and there in the mirror, laughing derisively at me, was the face of a horned beast. From the religious pictures I had seen as a child, I identified it as a demon. I could not believe what I had seen and heard. My face was the devil's face in the mirror!

I returned to conscious awareness, strangely disturbed. The mocking laughter rang in my ears and the horror of my Dreamtime was etched in my memory like a terrifying nightmare. Why? Why would my face be that of the devil? Was I so sinful that I had become the personification of evil? I shuddered.

I was so disturbed that I shared the last part of my Dreamtime with Jack. He laughed at me and said that I had been reading too many weird books. I was angry at Jack for ridiculing my passion for spiritual growth and frightened by my thoughts of escaping my marriage. I had taken a vow to stay married to Jack forever. I believed that I would be breaking God's law if I divorced him.

The thought of what lay ahead terrified me. Suddenly, my dreams of escape exploded in my mind as the horror of the pain we would undergo overwhelmed me. My Journey from Innocence had ended. My fear became the nightmare as the Journey through Hell began.

Δ Δ Δ

In looking back on this traumatic time of my life, I have often asked myself if my marriage could have been saved. The answer is yes. Jack and I still loved each other, although our love had stopped growing.

Jack would not change. To save our marriage I would have had to compromise my dream of fulfilling my life's mission. I would have had to sacrifice my pride, my spirituality, my sex life, my creativity, and my individualism. Staying in the relationship and trying to grow while Jack held firmly to his unchangeable beliefs would have been a lonely and bitter choice. The price was too great for me to pay. I chose not to follow the predictable path. To do so would have meant an agonizing death of my soul. I chose to sacrifice my innocence to undertake the journey into my soul, a journey that would lead me through the hell of experiencing my demons of shame, guilt, and fear.

We must each choose whether we will live our life locked into the conformity of the predictable path, or whether we will explore the uncharted territory of our soul. Many relationships change form when one of the partners chooses the path of growth, and the other adamantly clings to old beliefs and expectations about life and about their relationship. We must grow in our own way, and no one has the right to ridicule another's path. Such derision destroys trust and breeds loneliness.

As you examine your sexual experiences, it is helpful to write about your own loss of innocence. What were your first sexual experiences, and what sacred gifts did each bring? What experience was the turning point for your beginning the journey into your soul? When we can embrace all our experiences, even the most painful, as sacred teachers, we empower ourselves. Turning our woundedness into our point of power, we choose to no longer be a victim of our past.

PART TWO

JOURNEY THROUGH HELL

The measure of a mind's evolution is its acceptance of the unacceptable.

Thea Alexander, *2150 A.D.*

Chapter 10

Running Away from Home

It was our anniversary. Jack and I had shared sixteen years of marriage and nineteen years together. We had gone from love-struck teenagers to the most normal of married couples. We decided to celebrate the occasion by going to dinner at an elegant club and restaurant called The Constellation. After dinner we went home to make love, as was the custom for birthdays and anniversaries. We undressed and began caressing each other. Jack had been having problems maintaining an erection, so I used my hands and mouth to make sure his penis was hard. I wanted to have good memories of this night. He penetrated me and went soft. I tried to be patient, continuing to caress him. He was embarrassed yet pretended nothing was wrong. We had discussed his problem on previous occasions. I had begged him to seek medical advice, but he had refused, stating that it was my fault, that I was too pushy and demanding. He never asked why I seemed different, more aggressive. Nice people, even nice married people did not talk about sex, especially if they were brought up in fundamentalist homes.

This night had to be special. Maybe there would still

be hope for us. I was wet and ready for wild sex, becoming impatient as I manually and orally stimulated Jack's penis. When nothing I did seemed to work, he said he was too sleepy from the wine we had ordered with dinner. I went into the bathroom and masturbated, fantasizing about making love with the passionate Frenchman, Jean-Pierre. I rubbed my nipples until they stood out like pencil erasers. I imagined Jean-Pierre's passionate kiss, his tongue sliding in and out of my mouth, while his hands stroked my breasts. I imagined his fingers and tongue bringing me to orgasm. I pictured his naked body, with dark pubic hair curling around his penis. I hungrily sucked his penis until it was hard and throbbing. I fantasized what he would feel like inside me, filling up my emptiness, making love until we both orgasmed together with cries of pleasure.

I buried my face in my hands and sobbed from pain and loneliness. Afterward I slid into bed, staring at the stranger who snored softly far away on his side of the bed. The distance between us was an open chasm of unexpressed emotions. Some anniversary, I thought. I could no longer tolerate feeling trapped in a marriage that had stopped growing. The sexual passion and intimacy I craved did not seem attainable with my husband. Lonely and scared, I was uncertain as to what my next step would be.

Our daughter's softball team had a picnic the following day. Jack and Jackie greeted everyone warmly as they piled their plates high with Southern fried chicken, coleslaw, baked beans, and potato salad. I was not in a picnic mood and was too upset to eat. I had to talk to Jack, but he was talking to the coach and other parents, oblivious to my presence. I finally got his attention.

"Honey, will you go for a walk with me?"

"Why? The girls are just getting ready for batting practice. I don't want to miss anything."

"It can't wait. We can make this very quick, if you like."

"Okay. Let's go then."

We walked toward a dirt road, searching for privacy. Then I began. "I think you can tell I'm not happy."

"Well, I guess, so. I figured you'd get over it, though."

"I don't think so. This is serious. I've been thinking about how to tell you ... that ... I mean ..."

"Just say it!"

"I want a separation."

"You want ... a what?"

"Stop acting like you don't know what's going on. I want to be separated for a while so I can figure out what I want to do."

"To do?"

"You are making this awfully difficult. I'm not sure that I want ... well, you know what I mean ... to be married anymore."

"No, I don't know what you mean. Separation does not exist in my vocabulary!"

"I had a feeling you were going to be hard-headed about this. I don't understand your statement, 'Separation does not exist in my vocabulary.' What does that mean?"

"It's perfectly clear to me — either we're married or we're not. There's no middle ground!"

"But I need some space and time alone. Can't you understand that?"

"No, I can't. I'll tell you what you can do. If you decide to leave, just go while I'm out of town. We have plenty of softball tournaments this summer. Just leave me a letter. I don't want you to tell me to my face. I still think you'll get over this."

"Can't you face the fact that we're having problems? Don't you want to work through this together?"

"No, I don't. And we're not having problems. It's you that's having the problems. There's nothing wrong with me. It's you! You're never satisfied. You always want more. Well, I don't have any more to give. Whatever happens to our marriage is entirely up to you! I've got to go. I need to get back to batting practice."

The hurt in his eyes made a lie out of his cold, detached tone. I could not believe what Jack had just said. His words stung me painfully, yet I was not surprised. I had not expected him to be warm and loving, but to say that it was all my fault ... I began to make my plans.

Δ Δ Δ

Telephones that ring in the middle of the night always sound louder than daytime calls, more insistent and fraught with possible danger. The call that came at three o'clock was no exception. The voice said, "This is Catherine from the shopping center. Your studio is on fire. The police didn't know how to reach you."

"Fire!"

Few other words could have gotten us out of bed and dressed more quickly. Jack and I arrived at the shopping center just as the firemen were preparing to kick in the front door of my business. The health club next door was blazing. Smoke was pouring into my studio. I rushed inside to grab my business records, pushing past the firemen. They escorted me outside where I watched with tears streaming down my cheeks as they fought the blaze.

When it was over, my business had received smoke and water damage. I would have to relocate and refurbish. It would be like starting over.

Bleary-eyed, Jack and I went home and fixed coffee. A week had passed since I had asked for a separation. Neither of us had mentioned the subject again. I was waiting for the right time to leave. Over coffee, he said, "Well, have you gotten over your problems?"

"My what?"

"You know, are you feeling better about ... us?"

"How can you ask such a question? Did you think it was like a headache or PMS, and it would pass just as quickly?"

"Yes, something like that."

I rushed out of the room, tears blurring my vision. As I took a shower, I began to consider my choices. Could I ask Jack to move out? Yes, but he would refuse, because he considered this was all my fault. I would have to leave. Where would I live?

Most important, how would Jackie handle our separation? I had talked to her a few days earlier, and we had held each other and cried. "I don't want you to leave, Mom, but I think I understand. I just want you to be happy." I was worried about her. She was fifteen and getting ready to start high school in the fall. Would she want to live with me, I wondered.

She had read my mind. "I have to stay with Dad. He'll need me more than you. You'll make a new life for yourself. He would die of a broken heart if I left, too."

She was right. He would need her desperately. The two of them were so inseparable that I wondered bitterly when my daughter had become more important to him than me. I felt abandoned by Jack, but I could never blame Jackie. She was a perfect daughter.

After my shower I tried to sleep in the bed that seemed like a prison now. We had shared happy times in this bed, in this room, in this dream house we had bought together. I wished it were over, that it would happen quickly, painlessly.

The next morning I found the ideal location for my business. It was in a new building in a good section of town. The owner was friendly and agreeable to some decorating suggestions I made, so I decided to ask him about apartments. My face flushed as I stammered, "You don't ... uh ... happen to know of any vacant apartments nearby, do you?"

He grinned. "You see all these apartments next to the office building? You can rent as many as you like!"

"I might be interested in one, just one little one would do."

"The one-bedrooms aren't completed yet. But I do have a cozy two-bedroom. Why don't you take a look."

I was embarrassed. He must be able to tell that I was married and getting ready to run away from home. I looked at the apartment and loved it. The owner offered me a discount for renting two spaces. I took a deep breath and signed a lease on my office and the apartment at the same time.

Moving my business fixtures to my new location was easy. Jack helped me. I did not tell him about the apartment key that burned hot against my hand whenever I touched it. I kept waiting for the opportunity to leave. Meanwhile, I called a new friend, named George, and set a date for lunch.

George was single and flirted like he was serious. I had met him when I did some contract work for his company. Before I had completed my project, he had asked me to have a cup of coffee with him in the break room.

"Marina, I know you're married, but you really turn me on."

"I stay turned on most of the time, George." I blushed. Flirting gave me a rush.

"If you ever decide to run around on your old man, give me a call. I'd like to take you to a weekend hideaway at the lake and ... well, I'd better not say."

"You know I can't, but what did you have in mind?"

"Oh, lots of things, like having you wrap your long legs around my neck while I take you for the ride of your life."

His words thrilled my already overactive hormones. He was getting ready to kiss me when one of his associates walked in. "Uh-oh, look out, George is getting ready to move in for the kill!"

I had not seen George in several weeks and was excited about meeting him at The Constellation for lunch.

"Hi, gorgeous! Are you ready to accept my offer to go

out of town for the weekend?" He was playfully serious. There was passion and promise in his eyes. He could tell I was hungry to be loved.

"Well, George, I've been thinking about your offer. It's tempting, but I can't — yet." At first I had said no because I just could not have had an affair while I was still living at home. I would have felt too guilty and probably would have gotten caught.

"So why are you turning me down? You're not really, are you?" His boyish good looks made me want to say yes to anything.

"Well, I'm moving out."

"You are? Uh-oh."

"What's wrong?"

"Well, I don't know how to say this, but all that legal stuff scares me. I get real nervous ... Are you really moving out? When?"

"Soon. I'll let you know. You can be my first guest, sort of help me have a housewarming party." I was surprised at how easily I could talk to him like this. I shuddered at the thought of dating. Dating had little appeal for me. I just wanted to experience passionate sex.

There was an out-of-town softball tournament the next weekend. Jack and Jackie would be gone for two days. As soon as they left, I gathered my most important possessions: clothing, pictures, stereo, a few kitchen items, house plants, and my cat, Jopie, who was my best friend. I placed my letter on the kitchen counter. It read, "Dear Jack, You asked me to write you a letter rather than confronting you in person. Well, here it is. You have known for a long time that I have been dissatisfied with our marriage. I would like a separation. It's not just our sex life — there's more. I need time to figure out who I am and what I'm on the planet to accomplish.

"Maybe we can go to counseling to find out if we can make our relationship work. I certainly don't want to continue to live as strangers. We've had nineteen years together with many beautiful memories. I hope you will remember the good times and not hate me for what I'm doing.

"I love Jackie very much and wish she would come to live with me. She has asked to stay with you because she knows how much you need her. I know she's right, so I've reluctantly agreed to her wishes. If at any time you feel she would be better off with me, I would gladly accept her.

"Please forgive me for the pain this is causing. I wish things could be different. I will always love you." I signed it, "Love, Marina."

It had been two weeks since our initial conversation. I felt as though I had given my two weeks notice at a job, and I was walking out after nineteen years. It was a cold way to leave. Even though Jack had requested the letter as opposed to a direct confrontation, it was cruel to us and to our daughter. I felt as though I were taking a knife and stabbing our marriage through its heart. The horror of this analogy is that there was no blood coming from the knife wounds. I was killing a corpse, an empty shell that was no longer a marriage. If only we could have given our relationship a love transfusion years earlier. Perhaps a relationship seminar would have helped, or going to therapy. But now it was too late. The heart of our relationship had stopped beating.

Δ Δ Δ

I quickly settled into my new apartment with a few pieces of furniture borrowed from my landlord. There would be time to deal with household furnishings later. For now, I wanted to build my love nest and invite George over. I had started taking birth control pills a month earlier and was prepared for uninhibited sexual pleasure.

George was evasive when I called him. "I guess I can come over, but I can't stay long. I have plans for later this evening."

I had not thought about how many women he must have chasing him. Well, once he knew me better, they would be history!

Getting ready for my first boyfriend to come over was an occasion to relish. I lit candles, filled the bathtub with hot water, used fragrant bath oil, and told myself that my new life was going to be wonderful and exciting and free. I tried not to think of the letter I had written and of the pain it would cause. In fact, I tried not to think of Jack at all. Instead, I lay back in the hot water savoring the delicious anticipation of a new lover.

When George arrived, we sat on the sofa holding hands, while I outlined plans for the passionate weekend I had in mind for the two of us. He was nervous. "Marina, I like you a lot, but I've been caught in the middle of a divorce before. It's scary, with all the legal ramifications and emotional trauma. If you were still married, I'd be a lot more comfortable seeing you. For now, we'd be better off just being friends."

He left and my dreams came crashing down around me. I had never felt more rejected, abandoned, and alone. I cried myself to sleep that night. Somehow I had expected it to be easier to go to bed with a man when I was not wearing a wedding ring. How could I find someone to love me? I could not hang out a sign that announced, "Newly separated, horny, available woman, nice body, long legs — hungry for love."

Δ Δ Δ

The week before I had moved out, I had gone to see my parents to tell them what I was going to do. They were shocked. Mom had told me, "You know that it is God's law that you stay with your husband. Even if he were beating you, you would be required to stay with him." I had tried to explain to them what my emotional needs were, but they refused to hear what I was saying.

I went back to see them the Sunday evening after I had run away from home. My mom met me at the front door. I will never forget how she and Dad looked. Their skin was ashen, and they had never appeared so old and sad. Mom's words still resound painfully in my ears. "Jack was just here. He told us what you have done. I can never, ever respect you again."

Her words haunted me through many sleepless nights. When I most needed my parents, they were not available for me emotionally. Their religious programming condemned me, leaving me to feel like an outcast, a nonperson.

I felt abandoned, alone, wrong in the eyes of God, sinful, guilty, guilty, guilty. Perhaps my dream had been correct. I had seen the devil's face and it was mine. I wondered how I was going to find the strength to go through hell alone.

△ △ △

There are painful lessons hidden in the trauma of separation and divorce. Communication cannot wait until the last hour. Without open, honest communication, a relationship will die, strangled by distrust and fear. Relationships that are void of passion and intimacy imprison the partners in conformity to religion and the programmed beliefs that say, "till death do us part." I left Jack because our relationship was dead.

I am not suggesting that we throw away a relationship the moment it stops working. It stops working when we are no longer committed to making it into a vehicle for growth. Living in a dead relationship is like living in a morgue, whereas a relationship that supports the growth of both partners is vibrantly alive. It is a dance of joy.

Chapter 11

Hungry for Love

A week after I ran away from home, one of my best friends, Skip, invited me to spend the weekend with him in his new home in Dallas. Skip was a gentle, loving person who had told me for years that I was on the planet for a special reason. He had been my hair stylist and my special friend for twelve years. I treasured the hours we had spent together, having deep conversations about life and love, and about relationships. Skip had never given me advice about my marriage to Jack, but he had always been ready to listen and had encouraged me to believe in myself and in my dreams. I looked forward to seeing him again and sharing what I had been through.

Skip and I had enjoyed each other's company in the past, but I had always felt uneasy about spending time with him because of Jack's disapproval of his gay lifestyle. Now there was no one to frown at me for my choice of friends. I felt as though I had just escaped from a prison of my own choosing. We shopped in Dallas' most fashionable department stores, with Skip helping me to pick out a few luxurious items, including silk lingerie befitting of my new life. We went out to eat in an elegant restaurant and then to a disco, where we danced until we were exhausted. Spending time with my free-spirited friend was exciting, playful, and good therapy.

I even called my high school boyfriend, Darrell. I had heard that he had moved to Dallas, and I found his number listed in the phone book. I met Darrell for a drink at Reunion Towers, where we reminisced about our school days. We shared our life stories since we had last seen each other twenty years earlier. He told me about his relationship with his wife and about his children. He felt stuck in his marriage and had been considering having an affair. Darrell held my hand and occasionally touched my thigh lightly, saying that I must have come back into his life for a reason. I found his story boring, too similar to mine. When he asked if he could see me again, I told him that I would not get involved with a married man and that he had missed his chance in high school. It was a relief when he dropped me off at Skip's house. I kissed Darrell on the cheek and wished him a happy life. Although I was hungry for love, I was not desperate.

Driving home from Dallas, I wondered what new developments would await me. I thought about what it would take to convince me to return to my marriage. I could not imagine giving up my dreams of a fulfilling sex life. Jack would have to be willing to seek help for his problems in maintaining an erection. That would mean he would also have to be willing to take responsibility for his share of our difficulties. It was difficult to imagine his being open to change.

When I returned to my apartment, there was a message from Jackie on my answering machine. Jack had filed for a divorce. It had been eight days since I had left him. I felt shocked and hurt. Somehow the word *separation* had seemed so much softer than *divorce*. His hasty action left me upset and confused. I had hoped to have some time alone before having to make decisions about the future. Jack had never believed I would leave him. I considered his filing for a divorce to be his strategy to get me back.

I made an appointment to see an attorney and a therapist. The attorney assured me he would look after my best interests. The therapist asked me if I still wanted to be married. I did not know what I wanted. I called Jack and asked him to see my therapist. He said it would not make any difference. His mind was made up. I insisted that we go to lunch to discuss what we were going to do. He agreed, reluctantly.

Lunch with Jack was superficial. We hardly made eye contact, as we discussed safe subjects like the weather and our daughter's softball games. Neither of us was comfortable bringing up the subject of our relationship. Instead, we played our game of denial. After lunch we went to my new office. I locked the door behind us and took him up to the loft area. Then I tried to seduce him and failed miserably. We lay on the carpet while he tried one last time to please me. He did get an erection and began pumping rapidly to try to ejaculate. Before he could ejaculate, he grabbed his heart and slid off me onto the floor. His heart was beating wildly in the irregular rhythm that made him afraid he was having a heart attack. I tried to comfort him, but he pushed me away. He had to undergo his path through hell alone, just as I did.

I felt frightened of the painful journey that lay ahead. The person who had been my best friend for nineteen years had become an angry stranger to me. I went into the bathroom and cried. I repaired my make-up and smoothed my clothing. When I opened the door, Jack was leaving, clutching his emotional pain in his breaking heart. I called for him to stay and talk, but he ignored me. I knew then that we could never make love again. He had firmly anchored sex with me to his heart condition. I felt sad, mostly for the pain he was carrying beneath his cold facade. When we talked on the phone a few days later, I asked again if he would talk to my therapist. He said that he would, on one condition, that I pay for the session. I agreed. At this point I wanted a professional to say that it was okay for me to get a divorce.

After Jack's appointment with my therapist, I had one more session. She told me that my marriage could be saved, if I wanted to try to begin again, working through all the hurt and misunderstanding. Jack had given up. His ego would not let him fight for me, for us. I have wondered what might have happened if he had agreed to a separation and had given me time to myself. If he had believed in himself and in us enough to take that risk ...

During this time of confusion my parents were exerting pressure on me to return home to Jack, where they insisted I belonged. Mom admonished me by saying that I was breaking God's law. Then I received a letter from Dad. I could tell it was no ordinary letter. It felt heavy. I was afraid to open it.

I had never been much of a drinker, maybe a glass of wine with dinner, but nothing stronger. George had introduced me to Amaretto during our lunch together, and I had started mixing it with orange juice at home to help me deal with my pain and guilt. I downed six glasses of the mixture before building up the courage to open Dad's letter. I sobbed through the ten pages, loaded with scripture verses and warnings of the sin I was committing. He ended the letter by saying how disappointed he was in me and that I should get down on my knees and crawl back to my husband, begging for his forgiveness.

I felt as though my father were condemning me to hell. I could not imagine hell being any more miserable or lonely. My feelings of guilt and shame were magnified by my parents' behavior toward me. I had expected them to be sad and hurt. I had not expected the wrath of God to punish me in the form of their anger and condemnation. There was no one to comfort me. I could not let Jackie see my anguish. She spent one night a week with me, but I believed that she needed my strength, not my confusion and tears. Once again, I felt totally abandoned.

A few days later I went to one of Jackie's softball games. I sat out of view of Jack and his parents, who were visiting from Florida. I was too intent on watching the game to notice my mother-in-law approach me. She stood directly in front of where I was seated. "Well, Marina, are you glad you did it?"

I stammered, trying to think of an answer, "Did ... it? Did what?"

"You know what you did. You left my son."

I recovered enough to say, "It took two of us to make our marriage work and two of us to break it up. I did not do it to him." Then I turned and walked away, fighting back the tears. I fled to my apartment, where I sobbed in agony because of the rejection of a person who had been so supportive in the past. There was no one to turn to who would help me work through my pain and guilt. I had no close friends who had been divorced. I felt completely alone and wondered if God were punishing me for my sins with the anguish of abandonment and rejection.

Although my parents, my in-laws, my therapist, my religion, and my conscience all encouraged me to return to the safety of my unhappy marriage, I never seriously considered retreat. The taste of freedom, the thrill of a new life, and the challenge of fulfilling my life's purpose strengthened my determination to leave the predictable path. I knew that I would have to undertake the journey alone.

Δ Δ Δ

My first date was awkward and embarrassing. A friend introduced me to Brent who was balding, slightly paunchy, and drove a Lamborghini. I accepted his invitation to dinner because I had to get my first date out of the way. Okay, I also wanted to ride in his racy, fire-engine red sports car.

We went to dinner at The Constellation. First, we had drinks in the bar. Then we had a heavy meal, accompanied by an expensive French wine. Dinner was followed by coffee with Amaretto. I began to feel uncomfortable during the coffee and told Brent I needed to go home quickly. As I opened my apartment door, he tried to kiss me. I literally had to push him out the door, holding back my urge to throw up. I lost my dinner and all the drinks on the way to the bathroom, mostly on my silk pants. I was disgusted with myself, with life, and with being in my love nest alone. I was relieved to have my first date behind me and never went out with Brent again.

I started going to happy hour at The Constellation which was the "in place" that summer. Flirting with strangers over Amaretto on ice was a high. It was a comfort to have a place to go to forget my pain. It was there that I became acquainted with the man who would be my first lover. Bill was gorgeous — tall, dark, and handsome, with baby blue eyes that twinkled with merriment when he flirted with me. He invited me to lunch and I accepted. He kissed me in the doorway of my office when he came by to pick me up, and I fell in love. Lunch was a delicious blend of wine, quiche, and staring into each other's eyes and touching knees shyly under the table. I invited him to come over the next evening. I was hungry for love and hoped that Bill would be able to satisfy my cravings.

Our evening began and ended in my office. We sat on my love seat and held hands while we talked, and then our passion took over. When Bill kissed me, I felt as though I had never been kissed before. He awakened an intensity of passion in me that had been waiting for this moment. His kisses moved down my neck as he unbuttoned my blouse and began caressing my breasts. Soon we were both naked on my office carpet. His penis was much larger than Jack's, but I was wet and more than ready when he plunged inside me. He began to pump and pump and pump. Every now and then I was vaguely aware of a strange feeling of warm wetness on my back, but nothing was going to stop this ride. When he finally ejaculated, I held him tenderly, thrilled to be breathing the smell of sweat and semen. Then I felt something wet running down my back. The skin on my spine had been rubbed off, and blood oozed from the open rug burns. What a way to begin my single life! I wore those carpet burns with pride.

Bill and I spent many hours together making love, playing racquetball, and going dancing the summer of my divorce. He was separated from his wife and was also experiencing the pain of rejection and abandonment. We were good therapy for each other's loneliness. Bill was my romantic ideal in his appearance and in his lovemaking. His Southern Baptist upbringing had programmed him with the same toxic beliefs about sexuality that I had been taught. We discussed the sin of having sex outside of marriage and decided laughingly that it had been labeled sinful because it felt so good. Because I was in love with him, I did not feel guilty about our affair. I projected onto him all my ideals and expectations of the perfect mate, dreaming of what it would be like to be married to him, and how exciting it would be to make love as often as I wanted.

Being in love with Bill made me feel complete. Through him I experienced life as a glorious transcendence over the ordinary world I had just escaped. Each time he would call or come to see me I felt a thrill of ecstasy. When he did not call, my life was on hold, which happened frequently. Unfortunately, Bill was emotionally unavailable for me. Whenever we would have a deep soul connection during our lovemaking, he would become the dance-away lover, distancing himself from me because he did not know how to deal with his emotions.

At the beginning of our affair, Bill had said that he thought we must be soulmates, and I had agreed. He used to say we would be together whenever, wherever, however, forever, and I interpreted that to mean that he loved me. Once when we were making love, I looked deeply into his eyes and said, "Bill, what's happening to us?"

Panic filled his eyes. "I think we're having a good time, that's all." After that, he called less frequently. I waited by the phone and wondered what was wrong with me that I drove him away. He wanted to be with me on his terms, but the idea of love and commitment was too much for him. I continued to be in love with him for a long time, long after we stopped being lovers. There was always magic between us when we would meet by accident. I dreamed that one day he would be able to acknowledge my love. The only time he ever had the courage to tell me he loved me, he said it in French, *Je t'aime*. It was safer than saying the words in English. We were holding each other after making love. His words brought tears to my eyes, and I responded, "I love you, too." I was ecstatic. He really did love me! After that incident he stayed away for eleven days, and once again I felt broken-hearted and abandoned.

My lonely hours of dealing with the guilt and pain of my divorce often occurred when I would awaken in the middle of the night. I tried crying myself back to sleep but discovered that chocolate chip cookies and milk were a greater comfort than tears. I reconciled myself to the fact that Bill was not ready to make an emotional commitment. I would see him on his terms and at the same time look for someone else to love.

△ △ △

It was the day of my divorce, only two and a half months after I had run away from home. Jackie had asked me not to petition for equal custody. I had agreed, and it was a mistake that would be used by Jack for years as evidence that I did not love her. He claimed that I had left her as well as him.

I had two dates scheduled for my big day. George had called to congratulate me, and I had invited him to lunch. Bill was coming over that evening.

George brought wine. I provided the cheese and crackers. We ate lunch in bed, and spent most of the time with George having me for lunch. He had been giving me oral sex for a few minutes, and I was loving it. It was exciting to have a lover who was so attentive. I lay back and relaxed into the delightful sensations of his flicking tongue nibbling, stroking, and tugging gently on my clitoris.

George stopped abruptly and said, "Where are you hiding your orgasms?"

His question surprised me. I thought I was becoming an experienced lover, and yet I still was not showing any outward signs of orgasms.

"Oh, they're little ones," I lied. I was not even sure what an orgasm felt like. I knew what it was like to feel horny and lubricated. Orgasms would happen soon, if I practiced often enough.

My attorney called just as we finished having sex. Actually George finished, and I faked an orgasm. The phone call told me that I was a free woman. I felt relieved and excited. I did not deal with the pain. My divorce had happened quickly, almost surgically, as though it were someone else going through the ordeal. Jack had asked me not to show up in court. All the details had been agreed upon, and he did not want to see me in person. My attorney was there for me. I had fun in bed, instead, while I buried my feelings of pain and guilt in the enchantment of the moment. I felt especially excited to be celebrating my divorce in such high style. Two lovers in one day! This was the single life I had been anticipating.

That evening Bill came over, champagne in one hand and Haagen-Dazs ice cream in the other. I felt my vagina becoming wet with desire as we kissed passionately between spoonfuls of Pralines & Cream ice cream. My nipples stood out firmly through the lustrous fabric of my silk blouse. Bill stroked them gently, sending exquisite sensations up my spine. He took my hand and placed it against his bulging jeans. "Look what you've done to me," he grinned.

We went upstairs to my bedroom and undressed each other. I knelt and took his huge, throbbing penis slowly into my mouth. I flicked my tongue around as lightly as a butterfly, working up to sucking deep and hard, just like the Hoover technique I had read about in one of my books on pleasing your man in bed. Then we lay down together and Bill entered me slowly, deliciously. I raised my hips to meet his thrusts, moaning with delight. He was too preoccupied with his own experience to notice that I was not having real orgasms. I could not imagine what would make me enjoy sex more, but I was eager to find out what I had been missing. After Bill left, I began rereading my book on self-pleasuring. It was time to have it all!

Δ Δ Δ

"Mark, would you please spend the night and hold me?" I hated the pleading in my voice, but I could not understand why my new lover was in such a hurry to leave after the sex was over. I craved being held.

"I can't, Honey. I have to go home and let my dog out."

"Would you stay with me if you didn't have a dog to go home to?"

"Of course."

I knew he was lying. He was afraid of getting too

close. Yet Mark was good to me and fun to be with. He brought flowers and called frequently. I did resent the fact that he needed more space in our relationship than I did. I invited him over for Christmas Eve and fixed an elaborate meal. After dinner, instead of going up to my bedroom with me, he looked at his watch and said he had better leave. I was shocked. At least he should stay for a little loving. I tried to insist. I did not understand his wisdom when he replied, "This is your first Christmas since your divorce. You need to experience it by yourself." I had hoped that his presence would help me to deal with my pain. Instead, I would have to face my demons alone.

Tears filled my eyes as I remembered my first holiday alone, Thanksgiving. Mom and Dad had invited Jack and Jackie to dinner. Jack had cooked the turkey. I was invited over to my parents' for leftover turkey later that evening. I thought I had cried enough lonely tears, but evidently I had an endless supply. I spent Christmas Eve with no family, no sex, and no help from anyone. Sleep was the only tonic for my sadness.

On New Year's Eve I plumbed the depths of my despair. Mark had not called after Christmas Eve. I knew that he dated other people, and I felt abandoned because of his need for space. *Space* was the big word with the men I dated. I was worried that men only wanted me for pleasure, while I wanted more than physical sex. I craved being in love and finding fulfillment with the perfect man. I was hungry for romantic love, and so I gave sex, hoping to find love. The men I had dated faked romantic love in order to get sex. Afterward, they would dance away, back to the privacy of their hidden emotions, leaving me broken-hearted and alone.

I dressed in my glitziest designer outfit and prepared to celebrate the coming of the new year with the crowd at The Constellation. I was shocked to find that the club was nearly deserted. Everyone had private parties to attend. I ordered a drink and sat alone, conspicuous in my glamour and sadness. I left before midnight to bring in the new year alone.

Evaluating my life as a newly divorced woman, I felt little remorse for having left Jack. The sexual delights I had experienced since leaving home six months earlier more than compensated for the pain and guilt of divorce. I was unaware of how devastating it was to deny my guilt about having broken God's law and about being apart from my precious daughter. It was my parents' rejection and my ex-husband's anger and hatred that caused my deepest anguish.

Without a meaningful relationship with a man I felt lost, lonely, and depressed. I yearned for closeness with a man, an intimacy that included wonderful sex, but went beyond the physical passion to a deeper fulfillment. I had expected to be the life of my own private party by now. Instead, I had to dance once again with my old companion, abandonment.

Δ Δ Δ

Desperation teaches powerful lessons. When we are desperate for love, we will attract imbalanced people into our lives. I hoped that I would find Mr. Right to heal my pain. Instead, I found men who were equally wounded. I abused my body because of my hunger for love and acceptance.

It became obvious that I would have to hide my intense need for love and acceptance because it was a threat to the men I was attracting. My hunger for love was a raw emotion that drove men away. I needed to fall in love with myself, to connect with my Inner Soulmate. But first, I became an addict — a sex addict.

Chapter 12

Sabrina, the Sex Addict

"Hello, this is Sabrina. Marina isn't in right now. She's out having fun. Please leave your name and number after the tone, and she'll be delighted to return your call."

Sabrina began as a joke. I got the idea by calling a business in Dallas. The man I was trying to reach had a silly recording of himself playing the part of Jacques taking messages for Jim. I decided to have Sabrina take my messages.

Then one day Mark called and left his response. "Hello, this is Mark. I'm calling to find out if Sabrina would like to come over to my house and play."

What began as an innocent game eventually took the form of the projection of my behaviors that did not fit my religious programming. I did not consciously create Sabrina for this purpose. She evolved to become the personification of my addiction to sex. Marina had been looking for love and acceptance. Instead she got hurt when she allowed herself to be vulnerable. Sabrina had no time for love. She was wise as to what sex games to play and became an expert. She was ruled by unbridled sexual passion. Meanwhile, I buried my soul and my heart beneath a heavy load of pain, guilt, and shame.

Sabrina was sexy, uninhibited, and unashamed. She was wild in her insatiable desire for sex. She would walk into a nightclub and pick the most desirable, handsome, and intelligent man in the room. He would be her target, and she always got what she wanted. When she heard the lyrics to the Rolling Stones' song that included the phrase, "Make a Grown Man Cry," Sabrina adopted it as her fight song.

The games Sabrina played happened a few years ago, right before the time when AIDS became a known threat. Venereal disease was not a concern. I thought it never happened to nice people, and if it did, penicillin would cure it.

One summer evening the year following my divorce, I accepted an invitation from a neighbor at my apartment complex to go dancing. I dressed in a skimpy tank top with no bra and a full, cotton skirt. Jim and I went to a disco where the Friday night mating ceremony was well under way. The dance floor and bar area were crowded with scantily clad women and preppy men, looking macho as they scanned the selection of available women. I, too, was scanning the crowd while I tried to discourage Jim's heavy-handed pawing of me. I excused myself to go to the women's room, and on the way back I bumped into a man who looked like he should be my date for the evening. Sergio was tall with olive skin, green eyes, and a smile that said, I want you.

My first words to him were, "Where have you been?" Without answering, he took my hand and escorted me gallantly onto the dance floor for a slow dance that sizzled with the heat of sexual desire. He told me he was from California and would only be in town one more day. He invited me to his hotel room, and I agreed to call him after I got rid of my date. I returned to Jim and said it was time to go, feigning a headache. Safely back in my apartment, I called Sergio, whose deep, sexy voice suggested an unforgettable night of sensuous pleasures.

He was waiting for me, dressed in a dark blue silk robe. We kissed in the doorway, and then he offered me a drink. We sat down and began kissing passionately. He undressed me slowly, admiringly, and then led me to the bed where he began to lick and suck my toes, working his way up my body with his tongue. He took a small glass of Amaretto and dribbled a few drops onto my stomach and licked them off. More Amaretto and more licking followed as he brought me to a high pitch of arousal. I rocked my pelvis back and forth as he used his fingers and tongue to pleasure me. Then I sucked and licked Amaretto from his muscular chest and stomach like a kitten lapping up milk. His lovemaking was unhurried and flowing, as though he were playing a much-loved instrument. With Sergio, sex was a celebration. When he entered me, I wondered if I had found my perfect mate. I became more aroused with each different position. Before he ejaculated, he asked, "May I have an orgasm inside you?"

His attentiveness and creativity thrilled me, and I was ready to fall in love with this handsome stranger. We slept little that night, having sex two more times. At seven o'clock we ordered breakfast delivered to the room. Over my omelette and croissant, I asked Sergio, "So when did you get divorced?"

"Oh, I'm not," he replied unashamedly. "I'm married and have four kids."

I was shocked at what I had done. I had broken my rule of not having sex with a married man, but I was not sorry. Sergio had given me the most erotic night of my life. I stuffed my feelings of guilt, and Sabrina decided that sex, not love, was the game to play.

I gradually became more calloused about playing Sabrina's sex games. Another neighbor, Rick, had the reputation for having sex with as many different women as possible. When he invited me to his apartment, it was with the full understanding that there would be no emotional involvement, just sex. I visited him on four different occasions. Being with Rick was engaging in sports sex. There was no love, only lust. Sabrina had her fun, but afterward, the shame and guilt caused me to wonder what kind of monster I was becoming.

There was a birthday party at The Constellation that summer. Terri, the bartender, turned forty, and all the regulars were there to help her celebrate. The drinks were on the house. People took turns playing bartender, each trying to outdo the other in preparing exotic mixed drinks. After my third Long Island Tea, I wobbled toward the women's room. Rick stopped me in the hall, pressing his body heavily against mine. I could feel his erection in his tight jeans. He tried to unzip my jeans, but I resisted, running into the restroom. I had just closed the door to my stall, when it opened, and there was Rick, pulling out his penis. I could not believe he had followed me. There were other women in the restroom, but everyone was too drunk to notice or care. Without any foreplay, we had a quickie right there in the stall. I had another drink afterward, and somehow managed to drive myself home. I looked in the mirror at the face of a sad, lonely, frustrated woman. There was no joy in her eyes, only emptiness and shame. I had become a stranger to myself and an addict to sex.

I am not proud of having been promiscuous. It was something that I experienced as part of my search for myself and my search for God-man. God-man was my ideal. My friend, Leslie, and I had discussed our criteria for the perfect man. We agreed that we wanted to be treated as an equal in every way except in bed. There we wanted to be driven wild by a man who would take the lead in offering us multisensory sexual delights. He was God-man because he had a strong interest in spiri-

tuality and personal growth. My religion had programmed me to believe in a male God and in the importance of having a man be the spiritual head of the
household. Even though I no longer consciously believed
this patriarchal dogma, my reaction patterns were firmly in place. I would not feel whole until I had found
God-man.

I met the candidate most qualified to be God-man on
an out-of-town business trip. I was directing a project at
his corporation. Peter greeted me warmly and offered to
get me a cup of coffee. I remembered having met him a
few years earlier at a social event while I was still married. He seemed interested in hearing about my divorce.
We talked in the break room, and then he insisted on
helping me with my work.

At first I was too busy to notice that his interest was
more than professional, but the chemistry between us
soon became obvious. I thought of it as a light flirtation
that I frequently attracted, but it was more than a
game. The fire of passion burned in Peter's eyes when
he looked at me. He touched my hand, and I could feel
the passion in his touch. I felt as though we could have
kissed right there, but I pulled away. He asked if he
could come to my hotel room that evening. I agreed, and
after work I left to prepare myself.

I dressed for the occasion in white silk pants and
blouse, hoping that the white would help me look pure.
When Peter knocked on my door, I opened it, and for a
moment that felt like an eternity we looked into each
other's eyes. Then he closed the door, and we began kissing deeply, passionately, the kind of kissing that I had
read about and dreamed of. Slowly, deliberately, Peter
began unbuttoning my blouse. He kissed my neck and
my shoulders, and then my nipples which were erect
with excitement and anticipation. I lay down on the bed
as he removed my high-heeled sandals and unzipped my
pants. Slowly, sensuously, he slid them off. My lacy

panties still on, I began to moan with delight as he kissed and sucked until I begged him to remove them.

Then it was my turn to undress Peter. He was 6'6" with wavy, orange-red hair. I could hardly wait to see what color his body hair was. I was not disappointed — tiny curls of orange-red hair covered his muscular chest and curled around his over-sized penis. He was big and beautiful!

Our foreplay was a tender and passionate exploration of each other's bodies with our eyes, our hands, and our tongues. Peter was sucking my clitoris while he had two fingers deep in my vagina. Moving my hips back and forth, back and forth, I suddenly felt my body begin to move convulsively. I was crying and laughing at the same time, knowing that I was having a real orgasm at last.

Peter entered me in various positions of love play — on the bed, sitting in his lap, standing up, and with my leaning over so he could penetrate me from behind. I had never had such a passionate, loving partner. When he finally ejaculated, our passion had reached an intensity that demanded release. Afterward we held each other in wonderment.

The passion we had shared was different. There was a respect and gentleness, a depth of emotion in this man that carried me to new heights of pleasure. He told me that he thought that he had experienced the ultimate in passion but had discovered new depths of ecstasy with me. We both knew that we had shared a sacred experience. We had seen each other's souls and had joined as one being, physically, mentally, emotionally, and spiritually.

I was thrilled, except for one detail. Peter was happily married. He told me that his sex life was fulfilling and that being with me tested all of his religious beliefs. He confided that he had been involved in one other affair during his twenty years of marriage. I believed he was telling the truth, that this was not a line he told every woman he met. The reason I believed him was the guilt and fear with which he handled our affair.

Peter was a deacon in his Southern Baptist Church and believed that he was committing the damnable sin of fornication. We were together on four different occasions over a period of a year, and each time was more passionate than the last. He was afraid that our passion might destroy his marriage. I was afraid that I would never find anyone else like him.

We had a stormy parting in which he accused me of seducing him and being a temptress. I blamed the whole experience on Sabrina. It was her fault that I had become involved in this painful experience. Sabrina had no conscience. She was bad.

Δ Δ Δ

Time passed. I continued to hope that someday I would find God-man. I began reading books that opened my understanding of metaphysics. I read and reread Richard Bach's *Illusions, Das Energi* by Paul Williams, *2150 A.D.* by Thea Alexander, *Creative Visualization* by Shakti Gawain, *Pulling Your Own Strings* by Dr. Wayne Dyer, *Sidhartha* by Herman Hesse, and books about Edgar Cayce. I yearned for a relationship in which I could share my new understanding of spirituality. I no longer considered myself a religious person. I had stopped attending church when I left my marriage. Instead, I considered myself a spiritual person on a path of enlightenment.

I did not realize that I was addicted to sex. I floated from one unfulfilling relationship to the next, wondering if there would ever be one man who could satisfy me. I read a book about open relationships and decided that I would never be satisfied in a closed, committed relationship again. I had been divorced for two years, and no one whom I had loved could be trusted to be true to me. I gave up looking for God-man.

Then I started seeing Ray. We had met four years earlier at a social event and had talked casually on several occasions. I liked him as a friend but had not considered him a potential lover. He did not know that I had gotten a divorce until I called him to say hello.

We went out to dinner on our first date. I could tell he was nervous by the way he kept running his finger around and around his water glass. We spent the evening talking, and when we kissed good-night, I agreed to go for a drive in the country the next day. We saw each other almost every day for two weeks before we had sex. That was something new for me. I had decided to stop being so easy.

I was comfortable with Ray. He seemed like an old friend, someone I could trust not to hurt me. We spent hours holding each other and listening to love songs. When we kissed, there were no fireworks for me, no intense rush of passion that I had felt with Bill or Peter. But Ray was different. He was the first man who seemed ready to have a relationship with me that was built on friendship. Little did I know that he was as obsessed with sex as I was, and that he was projecting all of his romantic ideals onto me, making me his Goddess-woman.

Ray invited me to be his date for a banquet and dance out of town. When I arrived at his hotel room, he grabbed me, saying, "I can't stand this any longer." I did not resist his embrace. His loving was passionate and tender, and I could tell that he cared deeply for me. Afterward, when we held each other, Ray told me that I was his ideal woman, that he had been waiting all his life for me. He had dreamed of being able to hold me since the first time we had met. We made love again before the banquet, and I abandoned myself to wave upon wave of orgasmic delight.

Ray was the first man to love me unconditionally since Jack. Although I enjoyed his attentiveness and the novelty of being placed on a pedestal, his love over-whelmed me. His presence threatened my resolve to never again be in a committed relationship. I was shocked when he invited me to move in with him imme-diately. I thanked him and said that I was not ready to make that decision. I did not tell him about my inten-tion to have an open relationship.

With Ray, I experienced the holding I had craved for years. Our sex was exciting and wild. Finally, I had found someone who was not intimidated by my insa-tiable desire for making love. Yet certain things about him bothered me. He reminded me of Jack, except for the sex. We did not communicate well when we were not in bed. Although he had been raised in a fundamental-ist Christian home, he had discarded religion while he was in college. He was not interested in spiritual growth. He only read books on politics, war, and guns. He collected and traded guns, which made his house look like an arsenal. We had one thing in common, our obsessive desire for sex.

Ray had a fetish for sexy lingerie that suited the seductress in Sabrina. She would dress up in a black lace garter belt, seamed stockings, lacy bra, and crotch-less panties, and would abandon herself to playing the part of his mistress. With Ray, Sabrina was able to act out most of her wildest sexual fantasies.

Occasionally when I dressed up for him, I would look in the mirror and wonder who I was. The seductress, the temptress, the mistress, all of these identities fit the image that gazed back at me. I was feeding the addic-tion of a man who wanted to possess me and keep me from being a free spirit. He believed that I would even-tually marry him, and I heartlessly did not discourage him. I felt no shame and little guilt in allowing him to worship my body. I was addicted to the sexual pleasures of the moment, and I denied my religious programming that would have judged me severely. I had buried my desires for God-man and for a deep spiritual encounter during sex. Although our loving was passionate, I did not feel the intimacy that I had shared with Peter. I ached for the experience of oneness, the ecstasy that was my dream.

Ray did everything he could to please me. He loved to surprise me by fixing dinner in my apartment while I was at work. When I got home, he would have roses, a hot meal, and himself waiting for me. Yet all that our relationship provided was not enough. When he placed pressure on me to move in with him, as he did periodically, I panicked. Then I would go out with an old lover or a new one just to be sure that I maintained an open relationship. Ray knew that I was not true to him. He was hurt by my infidelity, yet he kept waiting and hoping that I would settle down.

We had been seeing each other for about a year when Ray decided to have an affair outside our relationship. I was crushed when I discovered that he had a new lover. What was okay for me to do was not okay for him. Rather than being patient for him to come to his senses, as he had been with me, I told Ray we were through and stormed angrily out of his house.

During our separation I spent many hours alone in my apartment, feeling rejected and abandoned once again. When I could no longer have him, Ray became more important to me. About six weeks later he came back. He said that he had dated someone else to make me jealous, to try to get me to commit to him. I was angry about the pain I had experienced and vowed that I would make him pay. I would make a grown man cry. This was certainly not an enlightened vow to make, and I am not proud of how I treated this special man who loved me deeply.

If I had started seeing Ray shortly after my divorce and before I became calloused and enraged toward men, I would probably have accepted his offer of marriage, security, and nurturing. Playing house with this sexy man would have been the answer to my hunger for love. By the time we started our affair, I had fully developed my addictive behavior and no longer believed I could be faithful to one man. No one man could satisfy me. I would find God-man by combining two or more men to form the perfect lover.

One day I decided to ask Ray why he loved me so much.

"Do you know the Greek word, Eros? To me, it refers to love of beauty. That is why I love you, Marina. You are beautiful — you are my ideal woman."

"But what about the beauty of my soul?"

"I've never noticed that."

With that comment I was certain that our relationship could never last. I felt that he looked at me as an object, like a prized work of art that he could show off to his friends. Now that I understand how he was projecting his fantasy of Goddess-woman onto me, it explains his lack of interest in spirituality. I fulfilled his need for a spiritual connection, and he could never relate to me as a flesh-and-blood woman. He would always keep me on a pedestal, and that was not fulfilling for me. I yearned for a deeper communication than we had, for a spiritual connection.

Ray and I saw each over a period of four years. Each time I broke up with him, I would eventually go back because I had become enmeshed in our codependent relationship. He provided a stability that was a safe harbor in my otherwise stormy life. I will always be grateful for his love, patience, and nurturing.

Δ Δ Δ

Being with Peter had given me hope that I could find a relationship that blended sexuality and spirituality. Peter had been vulnerable, allowing me to see his emotions and to connect with his soul. He had been unafraid to express the depth of his emotions, which was a trait I yearned for in a partner. I also dreamed of expressing my love in a way that would be free from the religious programming of shame, guilt, and fear that had imprisoned me.

From Ray I learned how to explore my capacity for sexual pleasure with a loving partner. He also confirmed my belief that physical, romantic love would never satisfy my deep longing for a soul connection. The fallacy of romantic love is that through projecting our ideal of perfection onto the object of our love, we empower that person to control our happiness. The ideal relationship is not with someone with whom we experience the roller-coaster emotions of being in love. Rather, it is with someone with whom we share a committed love and friendship, with whom we are free to undertake the journey into ourselves to connect with our Inner Soulmate.

I continued my reading and searching, never realizing that God-man was within me the entire time. Because of my religious programming, I was trained to believe that I would be incomplete without a man, especially a man who would be spiritually stronger than me and the spiritual head of the household. Hidden within me was the perfect balance of masculine and feminine energies. My search would eventually lead me back to myself and to my Inner Soulmate, but not before I had descended into the depths of codependence and abuse, a journey that took me through the dark night of my soul.

Chapter 13

Dark Night of the Soul

During one of my breakups with Ray, I met Tim at a business networking lunch. He fulfilled Sabrina's requirements for being physically attractive, intelligent, and good in bed. We talked a great deal about sex. Tim was insistent on knowing my deepest fantasies. He wanted to hear about my wildest experiences and what would most turn me on. No one had asked such probing questions about my sex life before. At first I tried to act innocent.

"I really don't have a lot of fantasies or that much experience," I lied.

"Oh, come on. I can tell a nympho when I see one. It's okay to bare your soul with me."

"Well ... okay, I admit it. I do enjoy making love."

Tim was inside me, pumping harder and harder. I was rising to meet each thrust, grabbing his penis tightly with the walls of my vagina, which was wet and ready for the thrill of coming together.

"Enjoy! That's putting it mildly. You love this more than any woman I've ever had. You adore it, say it!"

"Okay, you're right. I adore it! I adore it!"

We rode the waves of passion to completion and lay on the damp sheets afterward. Tim was still probing for information. "You must have at least one little unfulfilled fantasy. Come on, you can tell me."

"I've never told this to anyone, but since you're so persistent and such a good lover, I'll tell you my secret fantasy. I've been wondering what it would be like to have a threesome."

"A threesome? What kind?"

"You know, make love to two men at the same time. I might not be able to stand it, but it would be fun to try."

Tim said nothing more about our discussion, and I promptly forgot it. We made a date to go to the movies the following Friday night and kissed good-night.

When Friday arrived, I was excited to be seeing Tim again. Knowing that he liked sexy clothing, I took extra care in preparing myself for our date. I could feel the restless excitement of Sabrina stirring within me. My hair fluffed into a wanton look, makeup stressing pouty lips and bedroom eyes, I surveyed my closet for the appropriate outfit. Black was my sexiest color, contrasting well with my pale coloring and blonde, highlighted hair. It would have to be my black leather jeans, jeans so tight that putting them on could easily have brought me to orgasm. Their smooth texture felt luxurious against my skin. But what undergarments would I choose? I had never dressed in a garter belt for anyone besides Ray, but tonight a black lacy one with black seamed stockings fit my mood. Then I choose a black and red lacy camisole and French-cut, black bikini panties, all lace, of course. A black merino wool tunic that fit snugly over my hips was the perfect top. A wide belt that added even more emphasis to my hips, simple gold jewelry, and black suede high-heeled boots, my bitchy boots, completed my look.

Tim whistled approvingly when he came into my apartment. "You do look hot tonight, my dear! I hope I can live up to your expectations." He winked at me and led me to his sports car. "What would you think about skipping the movies and just going over to my house for dinner and drinks and whatever else you'd like to have."

I agreed with his suggestion. Tim fixed dinner while I tried to read a magazine. He would not accept my offer to help and said that I should sit on the couch and entertain myself. After dinner and wine he made Irish coffee, while I tried to shake the uneasy feeling that had been nagging at me all evening.

Tim brought the coffee and leaned down to kiss me, slipping his tongue into my mouth. We were interrupted by the doorbell ringing. There was a man at the door whom I had never seen before. Tim introduced his friend Greg from work. Greg sat down on one side of me and Tim on the other. We drank our coffee and engaged in small talk. I noticed Tim winking at Greg and wondered what was going on. Then I felt an arm slip around me. It was not Tim's arm. Tim jumped up to refill our drinks. My head was starting to feel light from the wine and Irish whiskey. Tim sat down, urging me to have another drink. He caressed my leg, running his hand up and down the smooth leather. "You certainly dressed for the occasion. Wouldn't you be more comfortable taking these off? They look awfully tight."

What happened next remains in my memory, shrouded in a fog of guilt and shame. Tim led me to the bathroom, where I undressed slowly in a state of shock mixed with excitement and some apprehension. I was getting ready to experience my fantasy, and I did not know how to handle my schizophrenic emotions. Sabrina, the sex addict, was lubricated and ready to take on two lovers at one time. I tried to deny my shame, guilt, and fear while the heavily fundamentalist programming of "The wages of sin is death," played around the edges of my mind.

I did look the part as I entered the candlelit bedroom

in my sexy lingerie. Tim kissed me, placing his hand against my damp panties. He smiled, "I think you'll be able to handle this." He removed my panties, garter belt, and stockings while Greg pulled off my camisole and began caressing and kissing my breasts. Tim used his hands and tongue to bring me to orgasm as I sucked on Greg's penis. Then Tim's penis was inside me while I continued to give Greg oral sex. They traded roles with Tim's penis in my mouth and Greg's buried deep inside my vagina. I allowed the alcohol in my system to numb me to what I was doing. Sabrina took over as I performed oral sex on one man while the other pumped me full of his semen. Then I got pumped again and again until I felt the tears spilling down my face.

"Please stop," I begged. "I've had enough."

Greg got dressed to go home and said good-bye. Tim asked me to never mention the experience to anyone since Greg was married. I was too ashamed to talk about what had happened to anyone. I asked Tim to take me home, where I showered and douched, trying to remove the feeling of uncleanliness from my body and from my soul. I sobbed myself to sleep, deeply ashamed of what I had done. I felt as though I had abandoned myself, my soul sacrificed to the excesses of sexual addiction. The face of the devil in the mirror was truly my face that night, the dark night of my soul. I felt dirty, evil, and trapped by my desire to drink deeply of the cup of life, including the bitter dregs.

When Tim called the next day, I asked him not to call me again. He was shocked, certain that I would have been thrilled to live my fantasy. I never wanted to see him again. His face would immediately have triggered my feelings of loathing for myself and for the fantasy that became a nightmare.

My religious programming of sin, shame, and guilt haunted me for weeks. I felt that I had fallen into a bottomless pit of darkness and would surely have to pay for my sins. I could not call Ray, although I yearned for someone to tell me that I was okay. I did not feel deserving of his love, nor ready to experience sex with anyone. There were too many painful emotions I needed to sort out in my mind. I was imprisoned by my disgust and self-loathing. It was difficult for me to look in the mirror without seeing myself dressed in red and black lace, a sinner giving her soul to the devil.

It was years before I understood the lessons hidden in this experience. I had violated myself by submitting to the excesses of sexual addiction. Sex without love causes deep wounding at the soul level. I experienced total alienation from myself because of my lack of self-respect and self-forgiveness. My descent into hell was an important catalyst for my reawakening. At the time I could not see the gifts in this nightmare because I did not realize that every experience is a sacred teacher. Flooded with guilt and remorse, I did not know how to save myself from the torment of my soul.

A few weeks later I met James who was to become my executioner. He would help me to process the burden of my guilt as he acted out his rage toward all women upon me.

Δ Δ Δ

Each of us has experiences in our past that have haunted us. The shame and guilt we feel represent our fear of our unprocessed emotions. Forgiveness is the key to unlocking these stuck emotions. Can you recognize your woundedness as a sacred teacher? You can release the pain when you are ready to forgive and love yourself. When we stop judging ourselves as guilty, we allow our journey of Sacred Sexuality to unfold.

Chapter 14

The Master and the Princess

Have you ever given away your power in a relationship? Have you ever projected your romantic ideals onto someone, treating them as a god or a goddess? Have you felt hopelessly trapped in a codependent relationship? A vital aspect of our journey of Sacred Sexuality is understanding the sacred gifts of relationships in which we have disempowered ourselves.

Δ Δ Δ

I had not dated since my nightmare experience a month earlier. Going to nightclubs no longer appealed to me. I had not even felt interested in having sex with Ray. He had called and left messages with my Sabrina message machine, but I had no desire to experience merely physical sex. There had to be a more meaningful relationship waiting for me somewhere. I decided to pour my energy into my business and focus on spiritual growth.

Everything happens for a reason. We draw people and events to us so that we may learn valuable lessons from them. I would be transformed by the rapture and the horror that entered my life when I picked up the phone, and a voice introduced itself as James Matthews. He spoke with a deep resonance that immediately drew me into its magical spell. He explained that he was a dance instructor and wanted to talk to me about using some of my office space. I was compelled to see the man with the voice that sounded mysteriously urgent.

In describing James, I wonder what possessed me to allow him into my place of business. He was shabbily dressed in brown polyester pants that were shiny at the seat, a faded polyester shirt in a red and brown, ghastly print, and black loafers that were scuffed and run down at the heels. All the warning bells went off in my brain when James put his hand out to shake mine. His brown eyes were flecked with golden sunlight. They locked into mine with hypnotic power as though to immediately take possession of my soul. I was mesmerized by his presence, and ignoring logic, invited him into my office and thus into my life.

There was an aura of tragedy that cloaked James in mystery. At first he spoke very little, and when he did, his voice seemed to be coming from the end of a long tunnel of darkness. Lines of suffering etched a face that was handsome when he smiled. He had recently moved from the Northwest where he said he had been the victim of a tragedy which had almost destroyed him. He had no car and no job and was living with his sister. Piecing his story together over time, I gathered that he had been imprisoned for statutory rape. He eventually showed me a picture of his fourteen-year-old girlfriend. He felt that her parents had been completely unjustified in pressing charges. I did not find out about this until later, until it was too late to extricate myself from his hold on me.

After James looked at my office space, we discussed his offer to give me dance lessons in trade for using the space twice a week. I agreed, and we set a time for him to return. I felt drawn to this stranger and was glad to be able to see him again. Two days later James was back, coaching a couple for a dance contest. I watched admiringly as he illustrated the dance steps, moving his lithesome body with catlike grace.

After the couple left, James gave me a samba lesson. I felt electrified by his touch as he guided me expertly to the beat of the sensuous Brazilian music. The suppressed passion in his eyes intrigued me, and I felt compelled to invite him to my apartment after my lesson. I wanted to know more about this man who was so different from anyone I had ever known. We listened to music and shared a light meal together. It was two o'clock in the morning before I realized it, and I invited him to spend the night on my couch. He did not touch me that night, although his presence had begun to cast a magical spell on me like an invisible net that would make me his captive.

Our relationship began with long hours spent listening to music, dancing, and sharing delicacies that I prepared. Homemade ginger snaps with orange-flavored cream cheese accompanied cheese balls and fruit wedges. These treats we fed each other by hand in my candlelit living room. The romance and mystery of this man stirred my deeply buried longings for God-man. As hours flitted by unnoticed, time became less and less important. I ignored my business, allowing my answering machine to take most of my calls.

The sexual energy between us was magnetic, even though it was weeks before we even kissed. Meanwhile I became so turned on that I called Ray and started going over to his house to satisfy my sexual desires. Although he was thrilled to see me again, the physical passion we shared left me feeling hollow. James had spoken of being celibate, and I was not ready for that. I tried to compartmentalize my feelings. I would share sexual passion with Ray, and spiritual stimulation would come from my relationship with James. In this way I created the perfect man, dividing my time between my desire for lusty sex and my desire for spiritual union. I did not plan to allow myself to be in love with either of them, just get my needs met.

Little by little my calculating hold on my heart weakened, and I fell in love with James, the mystery man in my life. Everything we did together had an air of celebration. His creativity demanded that an afternoon picnic at the lake be transformed into an elaborate ritual involving dance, music, and tossing me into the lake as a form of baptism into my new life. His flair for the unexpected constantly surprised and delighted me. We played childlike games in which we had to do three things we had never done before. He set the example by crawling up my apartment stairs backwards. With James there were no ordinary moments. He would appear at my apartment with a handful of wildflowers, reciting poetry to me. The first time we kissed made me forget all other kisses. His lips drew me into a place of ecstasy, intensifying my desire to make love to him, if he would ever agree to such sinful behavior.

I discovered too late that James was a radical fundamentalist Christian. He had seen me at the club I had frequented and had found out everything he could about me. He told me later that he had planned to do everything possible to possess me so that he could win me back to Christ. He would often state, "You are deeply loved." I thought it was his creative way of saying he loved me. Instead, he was saying that Jesus loved me. James believed he was doing God's work with me. He had other motives that were less noble, stemming from his rage against women. Later, when this rage would be aimed at me, it would destroy my world, ripping away my security like a raging river uprooting a tree and depositing it miles downstream.

Trying to describe his effect on me is like trying to capture the wind in my hand. I would lose myself completely in wonderment for days, and then I would be awakened by a harsh word or a cruel look from him. I continued to see Ray between visits from James, hoping that I could somehow preserve my sanity. James was livid when he found out that I was seeing another man. He did not call me for days and would not come to the phone when I called the house where he was staying. When I finally spoke to him, his voice was flat and lifeless. I innocently asked him what was wrong. He said, "I have spent the last week in hell." Hell was what he considered my infidelity. That was even before we became sexually involved.

I begged him to come over and said that I was sorry if I had caused him pain. I did not realize then that pain is never given — rather, it is chosen. He chose to be the most pitiful victim I have ever known, and I was so blinded by love that I did not want to recognize what he was.

He reluctantly agreed to come to my apartment. Heavy thunderstorms and possible tornadoes were in the forecast for that evening. As I hung up the phone, I felt the lightning an instant before I saw the blinding flash. The thunder sounded ominous, as though an angry God were threatening to take out His wrath upon me. A short time later James appeared at my door, soaking wet, haunting eyes burning me with their pain and unspoken accusations. I smothered him with dry towels and a tee shirt, which he accepted, and hugs and kisses, which he coldly ignored. He was angry with me and wanted me to experience his pain.

James had once said that his lifelong suffering had been so great that he should never have to work again. That alone would have been enough to get him kicked out of any sane person's house. By then I had lost myself to his control. I had fallen in love with my projection of romance and creativity, of spirituality combined with childlike exuberance for life. I lost myself in a fairy-tale world of high drama and tea parties. I spent less and less time at my business and devoted myself totally to pleasing the man who had become God-man for me. It is difficult to imagine that I allowed these circumstances to occur. It seems preposterous except for the understanding that the religious programming of salvation psychology had prepared me for this experience. I was programmed to believe that I was born a sinner, that sex was shameful, and that my spiritual connection to God would be through a man. Thus I became the captive of James' dark side. My self-worth during this time was at its lowest ebb. I was no longer in control of my life, freely abdicating my power to this practiced manipulator who preyed on women's emotions so that he would not have to financially support himself.

On that rainy night neither of us got any sleep. The torment of his soul was too much for me to bear. I knelt by the couch where he lay and begged him to respond to me. He sat up, fire flashing from his eyes. "All right! Then you must call me Master, and you will be my princess and enter into sin with no one again!"

"Yes, Master," I replied meekly. "What can I do to please you?" I could tell that this game was going to be different from any we had played before.

"Prepare a feast and then wash and anoint yourself with scented oil. Tonight you will pay for your sins. Then you will become my princess."

After bathing, I dressed in a silken gown and robe of pale blue, the blue of an icy mountain lake. My heart was beating rapidly, responding to the high drama that had overtaken my life. We shared a meal; rather, I fed him ceremoniously while he smacked noisily. I was allowed to eat only a few bites. It was part of my punishment.

James had brought a tape with him of heavenly music — the sound of doves, falling rain, and distant thunder — blended into acoustical harmony that set the mood for my night of total submission to him. He told me to lie down on the couch while he used the music and candlelight as aids to lead me into an altered state of consciousness. His hypnotic voice led me back through time to my birth. He asked me to speak of everything that I had done that was sinful or had caused pain to others. I moved forward through time, stopping to experience childhood incidents of shame and guilt. He kept repeating, "Yes, Princess, that's it. Remember how sinful you are, how vile. Remember that in spite of all your evil, you are greatly loved. Keep going. Tell me about your sins. Just how evil have you been?"

The game was no longer fun. I had been crying intermittently during my reliving of childhood experiences. When I reached my recent past and began to tell of the dark night of my soul, I broke down into uncontrollable sobbing. I confessed to having hated men and having wanted to see them suffer and cry. I expressed that I had given my body away trying to find love and instead had found despair and emptiness. Then he asked me about Ray, and I described our relationship as an obsession with sex.

He brought me out of my deep trance state, saying, "Do not open your eyes, Princess. Give me your hand." He led me upstairs to my bedroom and told me to remove my robe and gown and sit on the edge of the bed. I was still in an altered state when he said, "Now you may open your eyes." He stood before me naked in a dancer's pose. His athletic body looked God-like, shimmering in the candlelight. He began to dance slowly, sensuously, his dark eyes flashing. As he moved closer and closer to me, he commanded me to get on my knees with my eyes closed. I obeyed. He lectured me sternly on the dangers of disobedience for someone with my sinful nature. I waited, my heart pounding loudly in my ears. Then I felt something brush against my face, my lips. I wanted to peek, but his stern voice commanded, "Do not open your eyes."

"You may open your mouth, Princess." I did so, and

could feel a long, erect penis inching its way into my waiting mouth. Little by little I was able to get almost all of him down my throat. What followed was a ritualistic initiation into James' punitive form of sexual expression. I was not aware of the enormous rage that he had against women and that I had become the recipient of his unbridled emotions. The experience was overwhelming. I had trouble keeping up with his demands on how he wished to be stroked with my mouth and tongue. When he finally released his semen into my mouth with a loud yell, I felt as though he were pouring white, hot lava into my being. I kept my eyes closed the entire time, finally opening them as he crumpled onto my bed in exhaustion.

That bizarre experience bonded us into a master/slave relationship that caused everything else in my life to seem insignificant. For brief periods of time I would wake up to the reality of trying to salvage my business. I would return Ray's calls and spend time with him in the safety of his dependable love. My guilt and shame kept me away from Ray's house for weeks at a time. When I did have sex with Ray, I was petrified that James would find out. James was extremely jealous and would ride by Ray's house on his motorcycle to see if I was there. He always found out when I was unfaithful.

After seeing Ray, I would bounce back from the safety that seemed boring in comparison to the excitement of life with my master. James would return when I begged for forgiveness, and I would have to suffer through a period of celibacy before he would agree to be lovers again.

One night we went into the racquetball court next to my apartment where James prayed over me, calling upon God to strike me dead if I was unfaithful again. Then he prayed that tongues of fire would come down from heaven so that I might be "slain in the spirit." He asked that I pray in tongues. I felt nothing coming down from heaven, so I faked it. He was satisfied and ended the ritual by throwing me into the pool, fully clothed, then jumping in and making passionate love to me in the water. Such high drama kept me in a state of suspense and excitement. I never knew what James would do next. All other relationships seemed tame and boring in comparison to this man who could be a gentle lover one moment and an angry, punitive master who demanded obedience the next.

He had a penchant for oral sex. It allowed him to have me kneeling in front of him and worshiping his penis. On one occasion I completely lost track of time as I licked and sucked until he ejaculated his semen into my mouth. When I realized I was late for an important luncheon meeting, I hurriedly got dressed and drove to the meeting right through a speed trap. I was stopped by the policeman and given a ticket. When I next saw James, he assured me that I would be able to go to court and get the ticket dismissed. We researched every possible detail, returning to the street where I had been stopped, measuring distances that the radar equipment could have covered, and preparing my case. I appeared in court, defending myself. When it was obvious that the judge would not rule in my favor, I used the statement that James had suggested. At the end of my questioning of the police officer, I said, "Would you have stopped me if I had been pulling a little red wagon behind my car?"

The officer was completely disoriented. While he stammered and stuttered, trying to figure out how to answer that question under oath, I stated, "No further questions, Your Honor." Gathering up my notes, I returned to my seat. My fine was reduced from $35 to $10. I felt as though I had won. That one question completely changed the state of everyone in the court and put me in a position of power. My final question illustrated the outrageous creativity of the man who had taken over my life. It was unfortunate that James seldom used his creative genius for constructive purposes.

My parents and friends were concerned about my erratic behavior. I would set appointments and not show up. I was totally distracted and alternated between being deeply in love and deeply depressed. My master showed all signs of being manic depressive, and I mirrored his moods. If Ray had known the details of my bondage relationship with my master, he might have done bodily harm to James. Ray and I never discussed what I did with my life away from him, and there were never any questions about my unpredictable behavior. Ray assumed that eventually I would come to my senses and settle down with him. He continued to urge me to move in with him, but I knew I could never commit to the safe, predictable life he offered. I did value him as a safe haven whenever I tried to escape the bonds that held me ever more tightly to James. I did not know how to rescue myself from the emotional quicksand that threatened to destroy me. Hopelessly trapped in my role as Princess, I continued to play the game of bondage. I had no idea what lay ahead.

After I had made one more visit to Ray, James told me that I would have to be severely punished. He sullenly accepted the ceremonial meal I offered him. Then he told me to go upstairs and undress. Moments later he followed me and stood beside the bed. He opened one of the magazines on my nightstand to a picture of a beautiful brunette. He said he was going to make love to her while I watched. He then began to masturbate over the photograph. James' dark eyes were wild and out of control. I tried to resist as he forced me to my knees. My efforts to reason with him had no effect. I starting crying and begged him to stop. What had begun as a game of high drama became a night of horror. He became enraged and screamed that I was a bitch and would have to pay for my sins and for the sins of all women. The game had gone too far, and I was in danger. He held my head while he rammed his penis down my throat. I choked and sobbed in sheer terror as his violent thrusting continued. I thought I might pass out from lack of oxygen and from fear and pain. I was afraid that he might kill me, but his only physical violence was carried out sexually. He had punished me by violating and degrading me for being a woman.

My struggle ended as he ejaculated his semen into my mouth and all over my face. I stumbled to the bathroom and threw up. When I looked in the mirror, I saw the hideousness of his act in my tear-stained face. My eyes were swollen, and my hair was matted and damp from tears and semen. I knew that his hell had become our joint nightmare.

James stormed out of my apartment, and I was left alone to try to make sense of what had happened. I could not face thoughts of sexual assault and began making excuses for his behavior. I was too deeply in bondage to consider calling the police. There seemed to be no way to rid myself of this nightmare. I could not go to my parents. I could not go to Ray. My confidence and self-respect were nonexistent. I wish I could say that our relationship ended after that night of horror, but it did not. A few days later James reappeared, the gentle, creative lover I worshiped. We both acted as if nothing had happened. Denial is an anesthetic that postpones the inevitable.

The following week I made an appointment to see a Christian psychologist. It was as though the psychologist had been briefed by James. Part of my therapy was to memorize a chapter from the Bible, Romans 6. The entire chapter focuses on sin and includes the verse, "For the wages of sin is death ..." Instead of regaining my power to free myself from bondage, I was told that I should focus on sin, guilt, shame, and death! After two sessions I had heard enough about sin and decided to save my money. I called a friend who was a psychologist and also metaphysical. We did some healing work over the phone, beginning the process of rebuilding my belief in myself.

It was not easy to extricate myself from my tormentor. God-man had turned into a demon that had possessed my soul. He was spiritual in that he spoke of the beauty of my soul, while he tried to control and possess me. He was the most polarized individual I have ever known. One moment he was filled with childlike joy, dancing me into rapture. Then I would provoke him somehow with a word or lack of obedience, and he would become judgmental, vindictive, and hateful, punishing me as an angry master would his slave.

I now realize that James was my sacred teacher. This incredible experience was my choice. He was the projection of all my self-hatred and shame. He meted out the punishment that my religion of origin had programmed me to believe I deserved. When I used to dream of God-man, I had specified that he be the aggressor in bed. I certainly received what I asked for, and then some! Because I had hated men, I drew to me someone who hated women. This experience in religious and sexual abuse exploded my image of God-man. I would never again yearn for a man to play the role of God in my life.

Sometimes when I hear the call of mourning doves, I can still see his face. I picture us floating on two blue rubber rafts, side by side, carried by the lazy current of the lake near my apartment. The sounds of the doves cooing accompanied our ride on a mysterious journey. I can see the Master and the Princess, who caressed his ego with sighs and apologies, while her dreams of paradise were born and murdered in the space of two hours. He had a strong, lithesome body, lips that would melt hell, and glints of violence in his golden eyes. He entered my life like a subtle volcano, exploding my business, my relationship with Ray, and my beliefs into molten lava. He broke apart my world of comfort and the agnosticism that had grown into a hard shell over the shame, guilt, and fear instilled by my fundamentalist programming. I received personal evolution training at the hands of a dragon, part playful and loving, part fiery Roman candle that spilled hot wax into me. He cracked open my life with the force of a boulder crashing into my bed.

Because of James' insistence, I closed my business and moved to Tulsa, supporting us with part-time consulting work. Although the circumstances were controlling and manipulative, the move was a good one. It led to my eventually finding the career that would help me gain control of my life.

There are no mistakes. Losing myself in the hell of my guilt and shame, I gave my power away to my tormentor/lover who took advantage of my religious programming. When we choose to abuse ourselves, we will find someone willing to help us administer the punishment. Although it was an unconscious choice, I needed to overdose on shame and guilt in order to release the punitive programming of my religion of origin. This was part of my sacred journey. I was eventually able to regain my self-confidence and rebuild my life. It was a long, painful journey that lasted over a year. Its lessons will remain with me forever.

Δ Δ Δ

Religious programming of shame, guilt, and fear has its strongest hold on us through our sexual relationships. We project our feelings of unworthiness by drawing to us someone who will reinforce our beliefs about ourselves. We must examine our past programming and become aware of how it is affecting our experience of our sexuality. Few individuals undergo the obvious bondage of a master/slave relationship. Yet many relationships suffer from hidden bondage to toxic beliefs and to the idealized projections of romantic love. We can choose to free ourselves by refusing to stay stuck in beliefs that deny the sanctity of the body. We can choose to no longer project our ideals of perfection onto our mate. Where do we find God-man or God-woman? We find that God-being by looking within ourselves for our Inner Soulmate.

Chapter 15

Breaking Free from Bondage

The sunset painted the late afternoon sky with shades of red-orange, indigo, and burnished gold. I sat on the ground under the giant maple tree outside my apartment and stared through the colors into the endless Oklahoma sky. I wanted to die. It had been two months since James had helped me to move to Tulsa. There was little work for me, and my money was being drained by the expense of supporting us. I sadly wondered what had happened to my dream of creating a life of bliss in this new city. I felt the desperation of my entanglement with James. We were no longer lovers. James had decided that it would be best if we had an extended period of celibacy. There were daily arguments, mostly about Ray. I felt as though I were on trial. Every time James left the house he was paranoid that I would try to contact my old lover. I kept trying to assure him that I had left the past behind, but he refused to believe me.

During the weeks that followed, James' behavior toward me became increasingly cold and accusing. I no longer played the role of princess. I wanted out of the relationship but did not know how to break free. At last I found the courage to tell him that I could not continue to support him and that he would have to move out. My statements caused a violent reaction. James screamed that he could no longer be responsible for the safety of my soul. He grabbed some personal items, pretending that he was going to leave. I offered to drive him wherever he would like to go. He accepted, disdainfully.

Moments later we were on the expressway. I was driving fifty-five when he opened the car door as if he were going to get out. I slammed on the brakes and pulled over. He jumped out of the car while it was still moving and rolled down the embankment. I did not think he had been hurt, but his rage made me worry about my safety if he came back to my apartment. I quickly returned home, barricading the door with furniture. In the intensity of our argument I had forgotten to ask James to return the key to my apartment.

I wished that he would never return to torment me, that he would just disappear forever. I thought about calling the police but did not know what to tell them. Then I heard the key turn in the lock, and my heavy recliner started moving slowly. Wishing I had summoned help, I braced myself to handle whatever happened. It was James, disheveled, dirty, and cold from his walk along the expressway. Surprisingly, he had calmed down and tried to reason with me as to why I needed him in my life. He promised to find another place to live but assured me I would not be able to survive on my own.

James left the next day and was gone for a week. When I did not hear from him, I began to hope that he had disappeared from my life. Then he returned with a bag of groceries purchased with food stamps and the charming manner that had first enchanted me. His hold on me was still so strong that all my resolve to keep him out of my life melted with one passionate kiss. He said he was ready to be lovers again. I told him I was confused and did not trust myself to be with him. He promised things would be different, and I believed him. We had three weeks of bliss. James was attentive and adoring. While his lithesome body filled me with delight, his flair for the unexpected kept me living on the edge. After all that had happened, I had not expected to fall in love with him again. I was prepared to tell him that we were through. Instead, I allowed myself one more trip into fantasy land.

Three weeks later the honeymoon ended abruptly, painfully, with one phone call. Ray called to ask if he could come to see me. James had an uncanny sense of knowing who was on the phone. The moment he heard my voice responding to Ray's concern for me, James stormed out of my apartment. When he returned later that day, I had decided that I could no longer dance on the edge of my executioner's knife blade. It had become necessary for me to focus on reality and on regaining my sanity. I asked James to return my apartment key. He threw it at me and told me that I was condemned to hell because of my sins of the flesh. I firmly and persistently asked him to leave me alone. He left, but not for good. He kept trying to come back into my life by calling me and by appearing at my apartment. I considered getting a restraining order against him. Instead I secretly moved to a different part of town to rebuild my life and concentrate on finding a new career.

Breaking free from my bondage relationship with James was a long, painful process. The last time we saw each other, I was able to maintain my boundaries. It had been months since I had seen him. We met late one evening for coffee and then sat in my car talking for hours after the coffee shop closed. James apologized for assaulting me, although he did not use those terms. He did admit that he had taken out all of his rage against women on me that night and said that he was sorry. Then he began to cry and speak of demon possession. I held him while sobs shook his body. It seemed as though he were lost in hell, and I was at the entrance trying to lend him my strength to pull himself out of his despair. He clung to me like a tormented soul. It felt as though demons passed through his body on that dark night, but they could not touch me. I was totally protected from harm, especially from being ensnared by James once again.

After his crisis ended, James slumped over in a semi-conscious state. I drove to my apartment, half-carried, half-dragged him inside, and helped him lie down on the couch. I covered him with a blanket and went upstairs to sleep in my bedroom alone. The next morning he acted as though nothing had happened. I drove him to the coffee shop and kissed him on the cheek before he got out of my car. We have never spoken since. That was closure on the episode of the Master and the Princess.

Δ Δ Δ

I do not blame James for the things that happened. For years I had yearned for a spiritual connection, for God-man. My heart had been eager for spontaneous, romantic love. My religious programming made me the ideal target for his game of control and manipulation. My mother had often told me how important it was to be married to a man who would be the spiritual head of the household, who would be responsible to God for my soul. Although I no longer consciously believed in this patriarchal system of domination, the unconscious programming and reaction patterns had remained, making me vulnerable to James.

During the wild years after my divorce, I had not processed my feelings of shame and guilt about my sexual addiction or my rage against men. Instead, I denied these feelings. James was the ideal projection of all my guilt. He was a religious fanatic, a tormented soul who wanted to make women suffer. It was my unconscious choice to punish myself, to attempt to atone for my sins by becoming a slave to the man who fulfilled the role of my executioner. There were days filled with rainbows and dancing, ceremony and romance — a fairy-tale existence fit for a princess who was in love with a god. These days of rapture balanced the times of horror.

Breaking free from bondage, I was able to regain my inner strength. I can look back at this experience with gratitude for my growth. James was my sacred teacher of love and forgiveness. I have forgiven him and hope that he, too, will be able to release his shame, guilt, and fear programming.

Δ Δ Δ

This experience contains valuable insights for the journey of Sacred Sexuality. My bondage was an extreme enactment of the control and manipulation that many of us have undergone as a result of our programming. We must break free from the bondage that has separated us from the sacredness of our sexuality.

The programming of shame, guilt, and fear is religious abuse. It is an insidious form of abuse that generations of parents, ashamed of their own sexuality, have passed on to their children. We must break free from the bondage of our past conditioning and claim the ecstasy that is our birthright. The path of Sacred Sexuality is an important journey that can open us to healing the woundedness of our past. Thus we will choose an empowered future for ourselves and for our children's, children's, children's, children's, children's, children's, children ...

Chapter 16

Sex, an Interesting Diversion

My move to Tulsa had been a costly one. My savings were drained by the expense of supporting myself and James during the first six months. When my consulting work ended, I began searching for a new career. With no job and a dwindling bank account, I was getting concerned. I was alone and without a sense of purpose. I began to eat one meal a day, oatmeal for breakfast. That, along with some fruit and nuts, was my diet. When I was not searching for a job, I would lie in bed in my lonely apartment. Depression lay like a cold, damp fog upon my life. I did not know where to turn. After four years of single life, I again felt abandoned, alone, and emotionally confused.

My parents and I had reestablished our close relationship. They never knew the extent of my emotional difficulties, but suspected that my move to Tulsa had put me in a financial bind. They called frequently and sent packages of food as well as gas money to come to visit them. When the transmission failed in my car, they loaned me the money to buy a new Honda Accord. Having their support was a boost to my confidence and an affirmation of their love.

I felt envious of the people I saw in grocery stores, loading their carts with food. I was envious of people who had a job, any job. Hunger gnawed at my stomach relentlessly. I wondered if someone would throw me a rope to pull me out of my depressed state, but no one did. Friends called long distance, including Ray, who once again asked me to marry him. But I would not move back. I never considered retreat. I kept asking myself, Who am I? What am I doing here? What is my purpose in life?

One day as I was waiting to merge into traffic, I cried out to God in desperation, "Oh, God, please help me. Show me why I am here. What am I supposed to do with my life?" I had not been to church in years and had no desire to go. I did yearn, however, for connection with Divine understanding and wisdom for my life. I needed guidance and asked for help. I believed that somehow I would connect with my life's purpose.

It was not long before help came in the form of a suggestion from a new friend, Donna. She knew that I was looking for a job and mentioned the name of a company that offered adult self-improvement training. "You really ought to talk to the sales manager. He's a friend of mine. His programs help a lot of people and might just be a fit for you."

I called him immediately and set an appointment for later that afternoon. The office and classroom were impressive, and I liked the sales manager who was about thirty-five and dynamic. He invited me to dinner where I talked with him about my search for a new career and my desire to find my life's purpose. He explained the training programs and offered me a job in sales. Everything seemed like it would be right for me, until he invited me to dinner on Friday night. During dinner he told me that he had recently separated from his wife and tried to convince me to go to bed with him. That was a total turn-off. I had experienced enough sexual harassment to last a lifetime.

The next day I called him to say that I would not be accepting the job. He apologized for his behavior the previous evening and asked me to remain open and give the job some thought. A week later I called back and accepted the position, provided that he would never again make any sexual overtures toward me. He agreed, sheepishly, and placed an order for my business cards.

My behavior reflected my shift in focus. In the past I might have engaged in an idle affair with him. I felt as though I had a new perspective on my sexuality and on my future. After my detour through hell, I was back on my path. I no longer had an interest in sexual excesses or in allowing my addiction to sex to run my life.

I began my new career in sales with all the passion and purpose of entering a new love affair. I loved the thrill of getting people involved in self-empowerment and helping to facilitate their personal growth. I became a workaholic and hardly missed having a social life. My friend, Donna, expressed concern when I told her that I was having candlelight dinners alone in my apartment on the weekends. While I was eating, I sat across from a large mirror and talked to myself. I did not realize that this was the technique of affirmations and mirror work. I read books on selling and listened to motivational tapes. Within a few months my commission check looked so impressive that I photocopied it to send to my parents.

Donna kept insisting that I needed to find someone to date. Reluctantly, I accompanied her to a singles' night at a church that had the reputation for being the meeting place for prospective partners. I met Ted in the hallway on my way to Newcomers' Class. He asked me for my business card and mentioned that he would like to call me for lunch. I said that might be okay, if I had time.

A few days later Ted called, and I met him for happy hour in the lounge of a nice restaurant. We ordered a drink and appetizers, and before we began eating, I asked Ted if it would be all right if I said a blessing. Not giving him time to answer, I bowed my head, grabbed his hand, and said a quick thank you. I knew that Divine Spirit had answered my cry for help and wanted to keep the lines of communication open. While we ate, Ted told me that he was an atheist and an attorney. I was not impressed with either of his descriptions of himself. Yet he had a certain charm in a Yuppie sort of way. When we left the restaurant together, my car was parked next to his cherry red Porsche 941. I was underimpressed. In fact, I had learned to be wary of men who drove flashy cars.

Ted was persistent, and over the next month we went to dinner, to the movies, and dancing. He was fun to be with and expressed an interest in my career. I told him that I had recently ended a relationship that had been extremely painful and that I would need time before having sex. He did not pressure me, saying that he would simply enjoy being my friend. His kisses told me he was ready to be my lover whenever I would say yes.

The first time we had sex was on a cold, snowy night. I invited him to stay over after dinner. We sat in front of a warm fire and allowed our passion to take us from kissing to caressing. We undressed and stroked each other's naked bodies in the flickering light of the fire. I felt safe with Ted, allowing myself to enjoy sex again after the trauma of my experiences with James.

Our sex was good, but I never felt out of control. My passion was dedicated to my career. Ted would have to fit in as an interesting diversion. He was frustrated that I was so single-focused. He suggested that we would make a good team, if I could take some time out for marriage. I never considered it. I told him that I was fond of him but was not interested in a lifetime commitment. It was a new experience to be in a relationship that was not all-consuming. Sex with Ted continued to be a warm and friendly diversion. He was thrilled with my spontaneity in lovemaking and wanted to see more and more of me. I kept him around as a friend and a convenience. I still loved having sex on my terms, but I did not allow myself any messy entanglements — except for Ray.

Wanting to share the excitement of my career success with someone special, I invited Ray to spend the weekend with me. I had missed our passionate lovemaking. Ray bounced up the stairs to my apartment two at a time. He gave me a warm hug and a beautifully wrapped gift box. I opened it quickly, pulling out a rich burgundy colored gown and robe, with matching lace garter belt. He insisted that I model them for him. We closed the shades and spent the weekend catching up on each other's lives and having sex. Mostly we had sex.

After one of our lovemaking sessions, I looked in the bathroom mirror at an image that was foreign to me. In the past I had enjoyed feeling wickedly sensual and dressing up to play the role of his mistress. This time was different. The sex had been good, and the holding Ray gave me was tender. Yet our differences were more evident since my transformative journey. I felt the emptiness of physical sex and wondered sadly if I would ever be able to fulfill my longing for physical and spiritual union with one man.

Nevertheless, I was being pulled by the strong cords of codependence into wanting to spend time with Ray. Living in different cities helped me to keep some emotional distance between us. He wanted to move in with me and find a new job, but I resisted. I kept seeing Ted, comfortable once again with having two lovers who, added together, partly fulfilled me. Yet neither of them had the spiritual depth that I craved. I decided to forget my dream of the perfect man and focus on my career instead.

This was an important time for my personal and spiritual growth. My confidence regained, I knew that there were no limits to what I could accomplish. One Sunday I decided to visit a charismatic church that was well known in the community. I needed closure on the fundamentalist period of my life, and I received much more than closure. The minister spoke on a verse from the Bible that promised that your daughters shall return and be nursed at your side. His talk moved me deeply. My daughter, Jackie, had been going to college in Florida, living with her paternal grandparents. We spoke frequently on the phone about how wonderful it would be to live together. I felt as though Divine Spirit had given me a promise. A few weeks later Jackie called. "Mom, you'll never believe this! I got a scholarship to attend Tulsa University. I've been dreaming about being close to you again. Mom ... Mom, are you still there?"

I was too overcome by emotion to respond immediately. Tears of thanksgiving flowed down my cheeks as I embraced my daughter over the phone. She would be coming home soon to be at my side once again.

△ △ △

There had been many sacred teachers in my life in the five years since my divorce. I had experienced loneliness, codependence, sexual addiction, sexual assault, and deep despair. These were all part of my sacred journey. I was in charge of my life and excited about living my dream and sharing it with my daughter. I had survived my Journey through Hell.

As long as we wait for someone to throw us a rope, we will wait forever. One day, tired of waiting, we grab our own rope and pull ourselves out of our despair.

Do you recognize your journey through hell? It is the time when you felt the most pain and depression. Writing about the major lessons of this period in your life is a healing exercise. It will assist you in releasing your woundedness and opening yourself to fully experience your Sacred Sexuality.

PART THREE

SOULMATE JOURNEY

We're the bridge across forever, arching above the sea, adventuring for our pleasure, living mysteries for the fun of it, choosing disasters, triumphs, challenges, impossible odds, testing ourselves over and again, learning love and love and LOVE!

Richard Bach, *The Bridge Across Forever*

Chapter 17

Beyond Uncertainty

"**Y**ou are divorced, aren't you, Charlie?" The question popped out before I had even thought about it. I hardly knew this man. We had said hello a couple of times at regional meetings of the training organization we both worked for. Now I was engaging him in a conversation that made me feel as though I were on roller blades.

"Yes, I am."

He apparently knew I was single, or at least he did not ask. I continued, "Are you ever going to get married again?"

I could not believe the questions I was asking. In the past, I would have used forward questions to be flirtatious, but I did not feel physically attracted to Charlie. And besides, I was not interested in having a relationship with a man other than a partner I could see on the weekends to satisfy my sexual desires, and I already had two of those. Committed relationship? I had given up on romance, on finding God-man, and believed that it would take more than one man to satisfy me. I had sworn I would have only open relationships, which roughly translated into my doing as I pleased while my man or men waited around for me.

"Yes," Charlie responded. "I'm a gregarious person, and someday I will probably remarry."

"Do you have a list of requirements?" I continued to shock myself with my questioning.

"Only two," he stated. "Number one is she must be a training instructor with our company, and two, she must be my soulmate."

Charlie's answer stirred a chord of memory in my soul. Soulmate — nobody believed in such nonsense, did they? I looked into his eyes which spoke of longing for reunion and of ancient wisdom. I felt as though I had entered a time warp as I involuntarily responded, "Do you think we're supposed to be ... married?"

"I've been wondering that myself," he replied.

My logical brain rebelled against the possibility that this man was my soulmate. He was tall but overweight and walked painfully as though he had back trouble. Besides, I was through being a romantic. I had decided that romantics suffer too much, and I was not in favor of suffering. I would not speak of such silliness as a committed relationship. Yet I was compelled, and a bit embarrassed, to continue our conversation by inviting him to travel the three hours from Wichita to Tulsa to go to dinner sometime. I thought that would be a vague enough invitation to help us both forget our discussion.

"It's an awfully long drive for dinner, but I would like that," he stated. His warm, gentle smile expressed sincerity, but my left brain was convinced that he probably just wanted my body.

"We could have dinner and tell each other our life stories, and I'd like to ask you some questions about your business in Wichita."

"I'll give you a call," he said.

Charlie had asked me to read *The Bridge Across Forever,* by Richard Bach. I had agreed and reluctantly settled in to peruse it the next weekend. I could not put it down. I was mesmerized by Richard and Leslie's story.

Maybe, just maybe it was possible to find my soulmate in this lifetime. I had to find out more about Charlie.

Three weeks later he called. I was excited to invite him to visit me and suggested a Saturday a month away. I will never forget his reply: "I can't wait that long." We settled on a date two weeks away. I felt an anticipation I had not experienced in years. I had to explore the connection that we both felt with each other. It felt totally safe to tell him he could sleep in my spare bedroom. He said that was fine, but he would stay in a motel if I changed my mind.

At the time Charlie called, I was leaving to spend a week with my parents in a beachfront cottage in Gulf Shores, Alabama. I looked forward to enjoying their company and to having time to prepare myself emotionally for Charlie, for the possibility of opening my life to my soulmate, if he was indeed my soulmate.

Anyone who has spent time at the ocean knows its healing qualities — sugar-white sandy beaches, an azure blue sky that stretches into infinity, warm sun-lit days walking barefoot in the sand with gentle waves licking your ankles, time spent in conversation with loved ones, and time for quiet meditation.

I had not taken a vacation in years. Being at the ocean was the healing that my body and my soul had been craving, the renewal that helped me focus on the possibilities that lay ahead.

I decided to put my thoughts in a letter to Charlie. It read, "Dear Charlie, Perhaps someday we can share my love for the ocean together in this place. I am experiencing a complete renewal of body, mind, and spirit. The book you asked me to read has reopened feelings that I had denied, a yearning for the one with whom I have shared countless lifetimes, an eagerness to share the journey and fulfill our life's purpose together.

"I long for an understanding of our connection. Maybe we are soulmates and are destined to share our lives. I am excited to discover who you are, who we are together."

I added one last sentence as a normalizing disclaimer, "If we are not soulmates, at least we can be friends."

△ △ △

Charlie's hug enveloped me like coming home after a long absence. He was like a big, gentle teddy bear. We stared at each other in wonderment in my doorway until I finally remembered to invite him to come in. He had brought three gifts for me: a beautiful, Austrian lead crystal that transformed sunlight into a room full of rainbows, and two New Age music tapes. His thoughtfulness impressed me. Nice guys used to bore me, but somehow Charlie was different. He intrigued me.

As soon as we sat down on the sofa, my cat, Jopie, who never liked or even came close to any of my lovers, immediately jumped onto Charlie's lap. What is this, I thought, some kind of plot between the two of them?

We shared our life stories, talking over dinner and afterward for hours. At one o'clock in the morning, I showed Charlie to the guest room and went to my bedroom. Only I could not sleep. I kept wondering why this man who should be a stranger felt like home to me. Who was he? Did we really know each other from a previous lifetime, and was it possible that we could be soulmates? I had to find out more. Putting on my robe, I knocked softly on his door.

"Come in," he said, as wide awake as I.

"Sorry I'm late," I giggled to cover my embarrassment. He pulled back the covers. "Care to join me?"

"Okay." I entered his embrace and we began kissing. There were no fireworks, just gentle, warm and friendly kissing. Charlie had on faded pajamas — old-man pajamas. That concerned me because I had only known one other lover who wore pajamas, and I had divorced him. I helped him remove the offensive clothing while he slipped my gown off my shoulders. I had left a light on in the adjoining bathroom, and in this dim light we explored each other's bodies. Charlie's touch was firm yet gentle. He caressed me as though he already knew me. I released my worries about old-man pajamas when I felt the hardness of his penis pressing against me. We were both eager for intercourse. He penetrated me, and I began to move my hips in an undulating rhythm. I held back my orgasms until I could tell he was ready by the urgency of his thrusting. We moved faster and faster until together we released our passion, our fluids intermingling.

As we held each other afterward, Charlie grinned, "I'm glad we got that out of the way. Now we can get on with being friends." He explained that sex was vitally important to him, but even more important was our soul connection. In the days and weeks that followed we did become good friends and passionate lovers. I wondered if his theory that he called "beyond uncertainty" might be correct. He believed that our relationship was beyond any doubts and that now that we had found each other again in this lifetime, nothing could separate us. The love of soulmates is beyond uncertainty.

My mother considered Charlie steady and dependable, traits that would have sounded dull and boring a few weeks earlier. I was comfortable with him. For the first time in my life a man loved my soul, my eternal essence, more than he loved my body, although he did love my body, often and passionately.

Then he invited me to go on a short trip to Colorado with him. "Let me introduce you to my Colorado. We'll spend a week in Estes Park. I've hiked every trail in Rocky Mountain National Park. We can take the trail from Glacier Gorge Junction up past Timberline Falls, all the way to Sky Pond. You'll love it!"

Although I shared his enthusiasm for the mountains, I was nervous about taking this vacation together. Somehow it spoke of forever, which was a word that had caused me to break up with more than one man in the past. Could his promise of forever be different? Could the magic possibly last?

I told him that I would love to visit his Colorado. Then I started getting scared. The next day I called and told him no, using a weak excuse.

"Charlie, I can't go to Colorado."

"Why not?"

"I'm having a great sales month, and I don't want to miss my commission bonus."

Charlie was a good salesman. He would talk about the beauty and grandeur of Colorado until I would agree to go, and then I would back out again. I told him no six times, and he kept asking because he loved me beyond uncertainty. Without that theory, his pride would have stopped him from being so persistent. Finally, he quit asking. At the last minute, I called him and said okay and started packing. Although I was afraid of commitment, I was even more afraid of dancing away from my soulmate.

On our trip we discussed my fear of commitment. During the five years since my divorce I had become a dance-away lover, the trait that I had deplored in the men I had dated. Now that I had found the man whom I loved, the man who spoke of being soulmates with such certainty, it was time to face my fears and work through them.

Δ Δ Δ

An important lesson from the early months together with Charlie was to listen to my intuition. Our intuitive self will never fail us. At the deepest level of knowing, I had recognized Charlie as my soulmate. Then my left-brain logic took over, causing me to access my fear of commitment. It would take time and healing before I would allow myself to fully commit to my soulmate relationship. I would have to face my fears and learn to dance through them instead of away from them.

Chapter 18

Dance-Away Lover

The azure blue of the Colorado sky contrasted with the green-brown covering of pines on the mountains. The combination of the altitude and being in love made every detail of the surroundings fill my senses. We stayed in a tiny cottage on the icy, Big Thompson River, that sang a constant melody as it leaped and tumbled over rocks and boulders. I wanted to go skinny dipping until I felt the water. Instead, we used the river to chill our bottle of wine.

Charlie and I hiked and picnicked, shopped for souvenirs and attended a violin concert at the Stanley Hotel. I fell in love with the mountains and with this man who loved me for the beauty of my soul. I was thrilled that he shared my interest in metaphysics. We had read many of the same books and talked for hours about our spiritual beliefs.

Not all of our time was spent hiking and talking. We made love two, even three times a day, in our cottage and in the mountains. We could not get enough of each other. Sabrina had accompanied us, complete with sexy black lingerie and bitchy high heels. We played love games that culminated on my birthday with Charlie being my slave for the day. We spread whipped cream and strawberries on each other and then ate them. He prepared snacks and fed them to me. Then he gave me a sensuous massage, ending with passionate loving.

I was enthralled with this man who felt more like my soulmate each day. A few months earlier I had made a list of requirements for the man who had seemed like an impossible dream. They included: integrity, capacity for joy, loving, giving, confident, intelligent, poet, creative, open to growth, flexible, sexy, sensitive, expresses feelings, gentle, powerful, sense of humor, patient, fast learner, adores my daughter, and lets me be me.

This talented man wrote poetry that spoke of our soul connection. He adored Jackie and was a mentor to me in my career. I should have been in heaven. Instead, I drove home from our mountain vacation, nervous and scared. Although Charlie did not pressure me, he said that he wanted to spend forever together, one day at a time. I also knew that I had promised Ray that he could spend the next week with me. Charlie knew I had been seeing Ray when we met, but I had assured him that Ray and I were through. I agonized over how I could tell Charlie that I needed to have closure on the relationship that had fed my addiction to sex. I felt disloyal to Charlie, obligated to Ray, and compromising to myself.

Δ Δ Δ

There were roses waiting for me in my office when I went back to work, roses that were beginning to fade. Ray had sent them for my birthday. When he had called my office, the secretary had told him I was in Colorado. The day after my return, he arrived at my apartment angry that I was seeing someone else. We spent our week engaged in frequent arguments, making up only when we had sex. I felt the addictive power of our relationship beginning to lessen. Although there was a comfort and a security in what we had shared, I was not challenged to grow in the way that I was with Charlie. Ray's love felt shallow in that it only required the presence of my physical body to celebrate over and over the lusty, passionate games of sex that we played. With Charlie, I felt the celebration of life by being present physically, mentally, emotionally, and spiritually. He was inviting me to share a journey together as equals, a sacred journey of purpose and fulfillment.

When Charlie called, I felt awkward. I knew I would have to tell him about Ray, but I could not do so immediately. I missed my soulmate and the vibrancy of our relationship. I invited him to come to see me the next weekend. I hung up sadly, feeling hopelessly stuck, hopelessly codependent, hopelessly confused.

When Ray prepared to leave at the end of his week with me, he asked, "When will I get to see you again — or will I?"

"I don't know. I need some time to figure out my life."

He was angry and impatient. We played our familiar game of denial by not dealing with our issues. I was relieved when he left, but my torture did not end. I felt stuck in my addiction to sex with Ray. I also felt sad and frustrated that I did not feel free to totally commit to my soulmate.

The next weekend Charlie came to visit. He was waiting at my apartment when I got home from work. In my mailbox was a letter from Ray, and it was obvious from Charlie's behavior that he had recognized Ray's return address on the envelope. He was disappointed and hurt when I told him that Ray had spent the previous week with me. He could not understand why I needed Ray when I had my soulmate. I told him I had been trying to end things with Ray. His accusations stung me. "How could you see someone else after all that we just shared in Colorado? Beyond uncertainty means loving acceptance and growing through all experiences, but it doesn't mean I'm stupid. It doesn't mean I'm going to sit around passively while you continue to have sex with Ray. I won't share you with any man, and that's not being unreasonable. Make your choice — him or me!"

I was shocked by Charlie's explosion of jealousy and anger. I had expected he would react with pain and disappointment, but not with an ultimatum. In the past anyone giving me an ultimatum would have been history. I felt unworthy of the happiness I had shared with my soulmate, unworthy of the promise of happiness that stretched like a golden path into my future. I was stuck in my old programming, clinging to my pattern of dancing away when I seemed close to getting what I wanted in a relationship. My fear of commitment was a threat to my happiness. I assured Charlie that I would be faithful to him. Neither of us realized the extent of the pain we would undergo before I would be able to break free from my codependent relationship with Ray.

And then there was Ted! Before my relationship with Charlie began, Ted had told me he wanted to date someone he had just met. He asked that we remain friends, and I agreed. After my stormy weekend with Charlie, Ted called and wanted to come by to see me. I was glad to have an old friend to talk to. He gave me a long hug and tried to kiss me. I slipped away from his embrace and asked him why he was really there. He sheepishly admitted that he had quickly tired of his new girlfriend and wanted to be my lover again. I told Ted about Charlie and that I needed to give myself time to find out if I could work things out with the man who seemed to be my soulmate. Ted said that he understood. and to give him a call if things did not work out with Charlie. I felt relieved to have been able to end our affair with no hard feelings.

I was left with my fear of commitment to Charlie and my fear of releasing my addictive relationship with Ray. Two things occurred that helped me return to my path. I started studying *A Course in Miracles,* which helped me focus on self-love and self-forgiveness while releasing my addictive behavior.

The second occurrence was far more dramatic. Charlie had invited me to attend a sales meeting he was having in a small town near Wichita. The drive would take at least three hours. I left my office late because of a phone call from Ray who wanted me to spend the weekend with him. I told him that I felt confused and needed time to sort out what I really wanted. Because of my distraction, I took an incorrect turn and wasted thirty minutes. I knew I was going to be late and began driving fast, much too fast. At one point I was going ninety miles an hour over a paved county road. I slowed down to enter a town, thinking only about feeling stuck. What was I going to do about Ray? How could I free myself to commit to my soulmate? I despised being late and stopped impatiently for a traffic light. The next light was green, and I knew I could make it without having to stop again.

I saw an old Chrysler approaching the intersection on my left side. It was a dirty white, with a bent fender, and an old man with a straw hat at the wheel. All of these details are remarkably clear in my memory of that moment. As I drove through the intersection, the driver of the Chrysler kept going through the red light. Instead of swerving to avoid being hit, I froze in terror as I wondered if the answer to my dilemma was to die in an accident. I heard the sickening sound of crunching metal as the force of the impact buckled the driver's side and knocked my car onto the curb. I was wearing my seat belt, but I was badly shaken and had a sore neck. Somehow I made it through the police report and was able to drive my heavily damaged car to Charlie's meeting, by that time, very late.

Nothing happens by accident. I believe that I drew this experience to me because of my confusion and lack of focus. The impact on my life was to slow me down to evaluate my blessings. I was not seriously injured by the drunk driver who had hit me. My car would be repaired. My life was also ready for healing and direction. I felt willing to release my sexual addiction and step into the future.

Δ Δ Δ

Some people in my workshops express amazement when I tell them that there are no accidents. Everything happens to us for a reason. We create the circumstances in our lives so that we may learn valuable lessons. It is empowering to state that I chose at an unconscious level to be involved in a serious accident. It means that I am in charge of everything that happens to me. I was not the victim of a drunk driver. I was a volunteer for that experience. There are no victims, only volunteers.

This philosophy is only for those who choose to accept total responsibility for their lives. A young woman who had been sexually abused as a child became enraged at my statement about victims. She was horrified that I would say that she had chosen her abuse. I told her I could understand her resistance because I, too, had been sexually abused. Over time I have come to terms with the painful experiences in my life by accepting that everything is a choice. It has helped me to heal my woundedness to know that I am not a helpless victim.

The lessons in these experiences are important. Never avoid feeling stuck. It is always the prelude to true understanding. Welcome feeling stuck because it means that quantum growth is awaiting you. Wait quietly in the feeling of stuckness. Wait for your intuitive voice to give you direction.

It is impossible to run away from our fears. They will continue to haunt us until we receive their gifts. What was the gift of my fear of commitment? It taught me that I was afraid of success because of my religious programming of unworthiness. I was afraid of failure because of my divorce. I feared the depth of intimacy that I also craved. Being with Charlie helped me to see the beauty of my soul. I understood that choosing to commit to our relationship would mean choosing a path of intense growth, a path that called me to grow into my larger self in order to fulfill my purpose on the planet.

Chapter 19

Sabrina Banished

Have you ever felt that life was too good to be true? Have you ever had something so precious that you lost it because of your feelings of unworthiness? Have you tried to deny or suppress an aspect of yourself that seemed too wild and untamed, too threatening or out-of-control?

Each of us has a wild, untamed side that demands expression. This wildness is our creative, sexual energy. It is so vibrant and alive that it beckons us to explore our capacity for ecstasy. Yet a few moments of its expression can overwhelm us, leaving a hunger, a yearning to some day, once again, come face to face with our wildness.

Δ Δ Δ

"You're really good," Charlie used to say when we were making love. I would shake my head in embarrassment. I felt that his statement implied that I was wild and had slept around a lot. I had become an expert at what turned me on and also knew how to give a man sexual pleasure. Through experimentation in the art of self-pleasuring, I had discovered how to have deep, vaginal orgasms, as many of them as I wanted. Nevertheless, I tried to maintain the illusion of sexual innocence.

Charlie did not deal openly with his jealousy of Ray. He denied his feelings because he believed that our love was beyond uncertainty. He felt that soulmates arrived only once in a lifetime. Yet neither of us was sure that our relationship would last.

The weekend following my accident was a difficult one. Charlie's emotional pain over my week with Ray was tortuous. I kept trying to assure him that I had needed closure on a relationship of four years. I even told him how often Ray and I had argued and how much I had missed my soulmate. Charlie said that it was difficult for him to let go of the mental image of his soulmate in the passionate embrace of another man.

Charlie's back trouble was becoming more pronounced. He had a herniated disk that caused intense pain in his lower back and numbness in his right leg. The only time he did not feel the pain was when we made love. On that weekend we were making love for the last time before he would return to Wichita. I was not sure if I would ever see him again.

In the heat of our passion, just before Charlie was ready to ejaculate, I slipped into a deep vaginal orgasm, hoping to be able to orgasm together. Instead, as I was gushing my fluids, he was not able to receive enough physical stimulation to ejaculate. I was horrified at what had occurred. I measured sexual satisfaction with being sure that he had ejaculated. I felt that my overwhelming orgasm had been too much for him. I mentally blamed Sabrina for our problems. I felt guilty about her voracious sexual appetite that kept her from being satisfied with one man. At that moment I decided to banish Sabrina. In order to have a committed relationship, I would have to return to having a more normal sexual appetite. That way I would be able to stay faithful to Charlie.

I purposely willed myself to no longer have deep, vaginal orgasms, which had been my greatest joy in sex.

I felt that I was not worthy of such unbridled pleasure because of my infidelity. When I banished my deep satisfaction, I caused body armoring to occur. I unconsciously created a protective shield over my vagina so that I would no longer feel threatened by the untamed wildness of my sexual energy. I was unaware of the ramifications of this denial on my future sexual experiences.

Because of our love for each other, Charlie and I were able to survive the emotional turmoil of this time of adjustment. A few weeks later we went to Acapulco, Mexico, for a week. Our lovemaking was still passionate, but things were different. Charlie had made it clear that he did not like the lingerie fetish which had been the focal point of my fantasy sex life with Ray, so I dropped that. Also, I was going through some body changes that were concerning me. Two years earlier I had undergone a tubal ligation so that I would no longer have to worry about birth control. The surgery did not affect my enjoyment of my sexuality until I began taking estrogen. The hormone replacement therapy was prescribed by a doctor who had said that I would eventually need a hysterectomy. He said that all women should not be bothered with their female organs after they were through having children. I was gullible enough to trust this money-hungry butcher who prescribed estrogen for me, even though there was no apparent reason why I should need it. I took the medication for six months until I became disgusted and stopped, a few weeks before our trip to Mexico. It was in Mexico that I began having a period that would last five weeks. It was the last period my body had without taking hormone medication. I went into ovarian failure, which would eventually affect my ability to produce the precious vaginal fluids that had made sex intensely pleasurable.

Charlie and I were spending every weekend together. Our sex was warm and loving, although I missed the depth of orgasmic pleasure that I had banished from my experience. Ray continued to write and call, expressing his hope that I would come back to him. I told Ray that I had made a commitment to Charlie and was doing everything I could to make the relationship work. During the weeks that followed Charlie was offered the opportunity to move to Colorado Springs to run the training office for Southern Colorado. He asked, "How would you like to move to our Colorado?"

This time I did not hesitate. I said yes immediately and began the preparations for our life of commitment to each other and to our careers. I also made a final trip to visit Ray. When I called to tell him I was moving to Colorado, he begged me for the opportunity to say good-bye. I did not tell Charlie about the day I spent with Ray until years later.

I took a day off from work, planning to be back home by the time Charlie would call me that evening. My emotions were mixed — sadness about the final parting with the man who had idealized me and fear that Charlie would end our relationship if he discovered my infidelity. It was a pilgrimage that I had to make in search of closure on my past.

Ray greeted me with a hug that begged me to stay for a lifetime. He did not want to hear about my move to Colorado. He asked that we spend the day enacting our fantasy love life, pretending that it could last forever. His request seemed to be that of a dying man begging for one more day to live. I understood what I represented for him. I was his connection to his soul. He had projected his images of the idealized woman onto me, and I had willingly played the part. My love of high drama and my craving for passionate sex had found temporary fulfillment with this man, but he was searching for more than I could give him. I represented his other half and had the awesome responsibility for his happiness.

Our last day together was one of passion and sadness. Ray had bought another beautiful gown and robe as a surprise and asked me to wear them for him. I dressed in the luminous white sheer silk that felt as soft as a cloud. He was waiting naked on the bed for me. His eyes adored and devoured me as I slowly moved toward him. Gently removing the robe, he began to caress me through the softness of the silk gown. He buried his face against my breasts and sobbed, "Please don't leave me. Please don't leave me." I held him gently as a mother would hold her child, rocking him to calm his sobbing, while tears rolled down my cheeks. Then we kissed, wiping away the tears and surrendering to our physical passion.

He covered my body with kisses and buried his face in my pubic hair, bringing me to orgasm with his tongue. I licked and sucked his penis which pressed urgently into my mouth. He entered my vagina from above me, his tears falling unashamedly onto my body and onto the silk that I would never wear again. Our bodies moved in unison in a rhythm that we had perfected that would bring us to simultaneous orgasm. My legs were wrapped around his neck so that his penetration plumbed my depths. Together we climaxed with cries of release and of sorrow. My fluids mingled with his, as did my tears.

There was little to say afterward. We tried to share a meal together, but neither of us could eat. He stood on his balcony and watched me drive away. I was emotionally drained and yet relieved, believing that our love affair had finally ended.

On the drive home I contemplated the gradual awakening of sexuality that had been part of my journey. I had been unable to experience orgasm during my marriage and during the early months of my single life. I had learned about my capacity for pleasure from my different partners, culminating in being able to experience deep, vaginal orgasms, multiple ones. I had played with the fire of passion and believed it would consume

151

me, so I had decided to banish the wildness of Sabrina. It would be years before I would learn how to rekindle the flames.

Δ Δ Δ

The lessons in this chapter are vital for both men and women. Our cultural conditioning has taught women to be the projection of a man's soul, of his inner feminine, by being placed on a pedestal and playing the part of the idealized woman. Women are trained from childhood to be a mirror for a man, reflecting back to him his ideal. Thus we fall in love with someone because of the way they look, the way they make us feel, and because of the way they fulfill our fantasies. We play a role instead of being ourselves, especially in the expression of our sexuality.

When I found my soulmate, I found someone who recognized me as a whole person, not his other half. He refused to play the games of projection that would have placed me on a pedestal. It is the ultimate journey to retrieve our soul from its projection onto our other half. This sacred journey reunites us with our Inner Soulmate, the harmony of our feminine and masculine energies. Freed from our projections, we can join with our beloved as two whole beings. No longer searching for our other half in our relationship with our mate, we can dedicate ourselves to honor and serve each other in a way that empowers us.

There is a wild, untamed aspect of each of us that represents our raw sexual energy. We are programmed to feel shame, guilt, and fear when we experience this source of power. We feel out of control, overwhelmed by our capacity for ecstasy. Many individuals feel so threatened that they subconsciously create body armoring to protect themselves from fully experiencing their sexuality. The journey of Sacred Sexuality allows us to release our protective armoring, opening us to our capacity for wholeness and ecstasy.

Chapter 20

Fear of Intimacy

Moving to Colorado during the Christmas holiday season felt like coming home. Jackie moved with us, transferring her college hours to the University of Colorado. I would like to be able to say that life together as a family was bliss, but it was not. I brought with me my fear of commitment and my hang-ups about having fulfilling sex in a committed relationship.

The first household item we purchased was a king-size waterbed with a mirrored canopy. It was the perfect setting for two highly sexual individuals.

After the newness of playing house wore off, Charlie's heavy snoring started disturbing my sleep. His back pain intensified, which meant that he was coping by taking aspirin every four hours. One night I asked him to sleep in the guest bedroom so that I could get some rest. He must have felt rejection, but he said nothing about it and began making his bedroom separate from mine. We still got together to have sex, but not as frequently as in our dating days.

We were struggling to establish the training business which had been without a manager for five months. We lost money our first six months, although we worked day and night forming classes and teaching them. Yet the business excited us, and we enjoyed the challenges it offered. It was a thrill to work together as a team, helping people to empower themselves. In looking back at this time of transition into a new life, I have asked myself if I was happy. Yes, I know that I was. The love that Charlie and I shared was what I had been searching for. What came between us was our fear of intimacy, of revealing our innermost feelings in total vulnerability. Charlie did not trust me to be faithful to him. I also feared that I might someday dance away from him. We were in too much emotional pain to admit our fears, so we denied them.

Ray began calling me, and I would talk to him when Charlie was not home. We talked about how much we missed each other, especially our passionate sex. Ray asked me if I thought he should move to Colorado. My answer was evasive. I told him that I wanted to make my relationship with Charlie work, but that I was no longer sexually satisfied. On Valentine's day I received a card from Ray in which he expressed his love for me and his gratitude for our phone conversations. He was also explicit in his desire to have my long legs wrapped around his neck once again. I was out shopping with Jackie when the mail arrived, and Charlie opened the card and read it. I was devastated by his lack of respect for my privacy. He was heartbroken that I was still in communication with Ray. I decided to go underground. I rented a post office box without telling Charlie and sent Ray my new address. We corresponded for the next year in secret. Although I did not realize why it was so difficult for me to have closure with Ray, I knew he was connected to the period of my life during which I had been able to experience a sexual passion that was rapidly disappearing in my committed relationship. There was also the thrill of having a secret life and someone who was waiting for me in case I decided to run away. It was cruel treatment for Ray, and I desperately needed to come to terms with my fears.

Charlie's back condition continued to deteriorate. He could not move without pain. I worried that I was in relationship with a man who would eventually become an invalid. Out of desperation he began interviewing doctors and found a surgeon whom he trusted to perform back surgery. Presurgery tests showed that his thyroid was underactive, dangerously so. The doctor said that he would have had a stroke within six months if his condition had not been discovered. During the four hours of his surgery, I sat in the waiting room anxiously wondering if he would emerge a cripple. I prayed for his complete recovery. It was time to return to my path of rapid spiritual growth, time to build a life of bliss with Charlie.

His doctor greeted me with the okay sign when it was over and predicted a rapid recovery. He had no idea how rapid it would be. Charlie was out of the hospital in three days, and on the fourth, he was chasing me around the bed where he was supposed to be recuperating. The results of his surgery and thyroid medication were amazing. He began losing weight immediately, and within two months he had lost forty pounds. Instead of limping around from pain, he rapidly regained energy and strength he had not had in years. He was becoming the soulmate of my dreams.

I had been communicating less and less with Ray. He had told me that he was dating someone who wanted to get married. I wished him happiness and encouraged him to follow his heart. I knew that I could never go back to him. I still checked my post office box occasionally and was shocked the day that I discovered a letter addressed to me in Charlie's handwriting. I drove to a quiet street before opening the envelope. My hands were shaking as I unfolded the letter that contained a poem to me about the joys that we had shared and about the heartbreak of betrayal. It was followed by a short note requesting that we talk.

Charlie had discovered my secret, and I had no idea what would happen next. I drove home slowly, dreading our confrontation. I was also anxious to know how he had found out about my post office box.

I am amazed that two people who thought they were enlightened had to resort to such game playing simply because they had no skill in open, honest communications. I cried softly as Charlie told me that he had found a piece of junk mail addressed to my post office box on my dresser. He said that he felt shocked and hurt and that our relationship would have to change. He also said that he believed that I had left the mail in view because of an unconscious desire to be discovered.

There was little I could say in my defense. I told him that I did not want to continue any contact with Ray. The next day I closed my post office box and burned all the cards and pictures I had from Ray. I told him good-bye one final time in a letter. I thanked him for always being available when I had needed him and asked for his forgiveness for prolonging the relationship. I told him that we should both have the courage to give ourselves completely to our mates, instead of dwelling on the memories of the past. When I mailed the letter, I experienced a sense of completion and relief. It was time to focus on the present, time to heal my fear of intimacy. Ray called me one more time, two years later, to let me know that he had gotten married and was happy.

With the shadow of the past sent scurrying into hiding, Charlie and I began to spend more time communicating our expectations and needs. He moved back into my bedroom. Some of the walls of fear and denial had crumbled around us, and we renewed our commitment to each other. That was my first semester in graduate school, which began a time of intense personal growth. Our business was flourishing, and we decided that it was time to buy a house and put down roots.

Our problems did not magically disappear. There was still the issue of trust that Charlie would have to heal later in our relationship. I was still equating a committed relationship with routine sex. I had not had my menstrual period in over a year and agreed to a doctor's recommendation that I restart hormone replacement therapy. The love juices that had flowed so easily and deliciously while I was single seemed to have left me when I banished Sabrina.

Sex had become a responsibility, a requirement, and a duty. Although I enjoyed making love once we began, I rarely initiated sex and never anxiously anticipated it. Sometimes I orgasmed, but I often faked an orgasm to maintain the illusion of my satisfaction. I denied the feeling that our sex life was becoming routine. I missed the passion and wildness of Sabrina, the flamboyance of sex with Ray, and the creativity and high drama of sex when I was single. Charlie intuited that I was dissatisfied and that he was simply being sexually serviced. We rarely discussed our sex life. Because of our religious programming of denial we simply delayed evaluation of our situation.

Δ Δ Δ

Soulmates reconnect because of the lessons they bring to each other. Being with your soulmate does not guarantee happiness or fulfillment. It does guarantee that you will challenge each other to grow more than ever before. It means that the opportunity for heaven or hell is greater than in your separate lives. At each moment you both choose whether you will build or destroy your life together. Sometimes when your relationship seems like a beautiful castle, one fear thought or selfish act can cause your castle to shatter as though it were made of glass. Then you pick up the pieces and rebuild them into a stronger, more beautiful structure.

Our relationship can teach us many lessons in forgiveness. Forgiveness, according to *A Course in Miracles,* is the willingness to see only the good. When I see the good in Charlie and in myself, then I see our relationship as an opportunity for us to grow into our deepest remembrance of ourselves. We are here to increase our capacity to love and forgive.

Being able to relax and enjoy being happy can be difficult if you were programmed to believe that you should suffer. It is a challenge to feel worthy if your programming taught you that you are a guilty sinner. When we are able to release our unworthiness and our fears, we will be able to fully relax into the beautiful adventure of intimacy.

Are you afraid of intimacy? Are you afraid of revealing your innermost self to others, especially to your mate? The journey of Sacred Sexuality challenges us to break down the walls of fear and share ourselves in trust and vulnerability. Thus we will open a window to our innermost selves, an opening that can flood our lives with ecstasy.

Chapter 21

Rubbing Bodies Together

I picked up Charlie at the airport and drove home as quickly as the speed limit would allow. He had been gone for a week on a business trip to Portland, Oregon, and I had missed him. I had really missed him! In fact, the previous day I had self-pleasured in the shower, anticipating his return. We left his suitcase in the car and kissed passionately in the garage. He offered to carry me upstairs to the bedroom, but I raced him instead. We could not get undressed quickly enough, we were so anxious to make love. We jumped onto our mirrored waterbed and began touching and holding, kissing and caressing each other.

I had forgotten the mood music, so I stopped our foreplay to put on my favorite Kitaro tape. We took turns massaging each other to the lilting melody of *Silk Road*. Then we licked and sucked each other in a delicious time of oral sex. Finally, I could not stand waiting any longer and lay down while he penetrated me, and we began a wild ride to our shared orgasms. Afterward we held each other and basked in the warmth of our love. "I should go out of town more often," Charlie said.

I refer to this sharing of sexual passion as Western sex. It has predictable characteristics that most of us are accustomed to — mood music, candlelight, massage, kissing and fondling, oral sex, culminating in hard and fast pumping to reach climax. Afterglow follows with its feeling of having shared a special moment together.

Is there more? Can there possibly be more? Is it true that we are only loving at ten per cent of our potential? How can two people share themselves at ever deeper levels so that the sexual mingles with the Divine? What would it take to introduce our soul to our body without shame, guilt, and fear programming?

These questions did not formulate in my mind all at once. They developed through a time of increasing dissatisfaction with the highs and lows of my sex life with my soulmate. I began to experience a type of burn-out from genital sex, looking upon the hard and fast style of Western sex as merely rubbing bodies together. During this period of my life, I was meditating in an Eastern style of stilling the mind by focusing on the breath. It became comfortable to stay blissed out on a spiritual high, while making love did not feel spiritual. When I did have sex with Charlie, it seemed a little demeaning to be engaged in something so physical, so base.

Charlie was not happy about my lack of interest in sex. In order to maintain our relationship and to show my love for him, I engaged in obligatory sex two or three times a week. Of course, my hormonal problems were not helping our sex life either. It seemed that nothing would bring back my precious vaginal fluids. Even though we used a lubricant, I began to fear that having sex would be painful, as it sometimes was. Occasionally when we were making love, I could imagine Sabrina whispering, "Let yourself enjoy it. Let yourself go!"

I felt stuck, but I saw no solution other than to continue to play a game that no longer turned me on. I dreamed of finding a gentler way of making love but did not know where to turn. Then one day I read a magazine article that mentioned Tantra as a spiritual approach to sexuality. I rushed to the bookstore and purchased three books on the subject. I was fascinated with the philosophy of sex as a doorway to experiencing the Divine. I had been using meditation for that purpose and was excited at the possibility of sharing divine sexual ecstasy with my soulmate.

Charlie was camping alone in the mountains on his annual retreat. I could not wait for him to return. I put on my hiking boots and day pack and began the trek up Pike's Peak to find him. About seven miles up Barr Trail we met, and I began kissing him passionately. He was more surprised than passionate. I was the one who led the way down the mountain at a rapid pace. I had prepared a sacred space in our bedroom with soft rugs and pillows on the floor, fresh flowers in a crystal vase, fragrant candles, and my Tantra books nearby. Charlie was tired and sweaty from his days of trekking. He had not expected to be ambushed by a sexy soulmate and had trouble understanding my excited and rather distorted description of what I wanted to explore together.

"Divine sex? Sounds like an oxymoron to me," he joked.

Our first attempt at Tantric loving was awkward. When I tried to explain the breathing methods, Charlie acted more interested in taking a nap. I ignored the fact that he had spent the last week hiking and camping at high altitude and kept trying to convince him to join my excitement. While he slept, I practiced sexual breathing. I decided to ease Charlie into this new approach a bit more gently.

Charlie agreed to read one of my books, *Tantra: The Art of Conscious Loving,* by Charles and Caroline Muir. It provided him with a basic understanding of Tantra for Western lovers. It helped to open our communication and Charlie's understanding of my sexual frustration.

We adapted some of the exercises into our sex life, but our focus still seemed too goal oriented. I yearned for a deeper intimacy between us. Although I continued to study Tantra, other than occasional moments of bliss, our sex life still seemed routine. After several months had passed, Charlie began to complain that he was getting more sex before Tantra. He said that he was having problems with his expectations of our relationship and wished that he had met me during my wild and sexy Sabrina days, before I became so preoccupied with divine sex.

Tantric loving fulfills me because its focus is non-goal oriented, and it provides me with a soul communion with my mate. Most people are familiar with the Ann Landers survey in which women were asked, "If you were given a choice, would you prefer cuddling or sexual intercourse?" Of the 90,000 respondents, over 64,000 women said that they would prefer cuddling. The survey results show an overwhelming lack of fulfillment in Western sex for two-thirds of all women. The gentle, slow loving I was studying provided intimacy without the need to possess.

Sexual frustration is often the result of the basic differences between men and women. Men can be compared to the energy of fire and women to the energy of water. Men are more easily aroused, burning hot with the flames of passion, and then those flames quickly go out with ejaculation. Their experience of sex is often a genital one because the genitals are the center of sexual passion.

On the other hand, women take longer to become aroused, similar to the process of bringing water to a boil. When a woman reaches full arousal, she can remain in that state for long periods of time, experiencing multiple orgasms. However, a woman's experience of her sexuality is an experience of the heart. Her desire for intimacy and spiritual union often leads to dissatisfaction in her relationship.

My study of Tantra taught me that we are totally responsible for our own sexual pleasure and fulfillment. We have been programmed to believe that our mate should know exactly how to fulfill our needs. It is empowering to take responsibility for our own ecstasy. Yet there can be a conflict between meeting our needs and wanting to show love to our mate. Charlie's complaint had been that he had never felt he could get enough sex in a relationship. He called himself oversexed and used the analogy of sitting down to a meal and having a plate that was never quite full enough for his appetite.

As I was working on this book, I noticed that all our issues began to surface so that I could deal with them as part of this sacred journey. Early one morning after I had gotten up to meditate, Charlie invited me to come back to bed just to cuddle. I agreed and discovered his erection waiting for me. I had a passionate lover on my hands and was not interested in servicing his needs. Yet I loved him and wanted to see him happy. I was caught in a dilemma. Did I have sex and deny my needs, or did I explain my needs and leave him to handle his own erection. This incident caused me to suggest that maybe I was the wrong mate for him. He suggested that perhaps he was not a good enough lover to turn me on.

During this same time period I was having bodywork done by a male massage therapist. I did not realize it when I began the therapy, but Charlie had not healed his trust issues with me. He became obsessive about my massage appointments, wanting to know how much of my clothing I removed. Then he suggested that I was flaunting my breasts and enjoying titillating the therapist. I was horrified. I had no idea that he was harboring such fear and resentment. I allowed my ego to get involved and asked him how he dared to tell me what I could do with my body. How dared he act as though he owned my body! He blamed it all on his Southern Baptist programming and said that he knew he was being illogical. Nevertheless, the battle lines had been drawn, and we began to argue about our sex life. I kept repeating that we were practicing extremely unenlightened behavior. At times we were able to laugh about our issues. At other times we held each other and cried. I had just completed writing the Journey through Hell, and Charlie had been reading about my sexual experiences when I was single. He was already familiar with some of them, but it was painful for him to read the details. My body responded to the releasing process by having three weeks of diarrhea. We were a mess! And I only undertake projects that scare me!

We seemed hopelessly stuck. I called a friend who does energy work and had her help us to move through our extreme polarization. Polarization occurs when we take opposing sides. It is the opposite of oneness. Our friend helped us to release our past programming, which she called blueprints. She told us that we could choose whether we wanted to accept a new blueprint for our relationship or take back the old one that had kept us stuck. I felt as though a professional moving company had packed all our old beliefs and reaction patterns and had moved them out of our relationship. Some of our beliefs were still in a mythical front yard, waiting to be loaded into the moving van. In the next two days we went through our issues at light speed. Every unresolved conflict we had ever denied, surfaced. I had the image of going through our boxes in the front yard, pulling out the belief systems and reaction patterns that we had outgrown, and trying them on one last time. At one point in our crisis I asked Charlie if he was going to apologize for his statements about my flaunting my breasts. He responded by asking me if I had ever said I was sorry about what had happened with Ray many years earlier. I was stunned! Our egos were at war, and the pain was too intense. I asked for a time-out, and Charlie went to see a movie.

While he was gone, I prayed for a miracle. Then I noticed a book I had bought the month before. I spent the afternoon reading *A Return to Love* by Marianne Williamson. Her book is based on *A Course in Miracles* and offers some profound insights, particularly concerning relationships. She calls a miracle a "shift in perception." By the end of the afternoon, my miracle was beginning.

I teach the fact that we are here to serve, and I had been forgetting to live what I teach. I had been so concerned about being divine lovers that I had neglected many opportunities to experience divine love in my relationship with my beloved. Charlie is a man who gives constantly, a caretaker with a good balance of masculine and feminine energy. I had become out of balance in my masculine energy to the point of neglecting to show my love for Charlie in ways that nurtured him. By focusing exclusively on what I needed, I had been ignoring his needs.

I once told my friend Michelle that I wished Charlie would catch up with my rate of growth. Why was he not more like me? She said that I was not more evolved than Charlie. He was simply different. That did not make him wrong. When we think of life as a sacred circle, then there is no linear progression. All paths lead to truth. My experience of my path does not control his experience of his path. I had been trying to make Charlie be like me, and it had not been working. I had lost sight of my purpose in our relationship — to serve in a way that promoted the maximum growth of us both.

I was deeply touched by Marianne Williamson's reference to forgiveness as the selective remembering of only the loving experiences. When we practice radical forgiveness, we completely let go of the past. These were things that I knew but had neglected to put into practice. I could hardly wait for Charlie to come home to share my insights with him.

He had gone to three movies. As soon as he walked in the door, we began discussing our conflict, and I shared the insights I had received from my reading. I still felt wounded by Charlie's accusations. We discussed his trust issue, and he said that he was not sure he could ever trust me completely. My ego reacted, "You mean that all these years of being perfectly trustworthy mean nothing to you? I don't know if I can be in relationship with someone who doesn't trust me!"

I waited for him to mention my breasts again, and he did not disappoint me. He even repeated the word *flaunt*. When he did, I pulled up my sweatshirt and marched around our motor home, screaming at him that having a massage was not considered flaunting your breasts except by assholes. After my outburst, we were silent. Then Charlie said, "I wish I could do that, be intense like that." We started laughing, and the crisis was over.

During the entire experience I kept looking for the gift, knowing that there were lessons hidden in the pain. The next morning I sat outside for my meditation and received the understanding that made the miracle shift in perception. A relationship works when we stop projecting our expectations onto our mate. We need to encourage our mate to grow in whatever way he chooses. Perhaps Tantric love was not as important to Charlie as it was to me. I could share myself in a Tantric way while he experienced genital sex. He was still giving me love, abundantly.

Another shift in perception was that I wanted Charlie's plate to be full to overflowing. I wanted him to experience as much sex with me as he liked. That did not mean that I would always be available to the point of denying my needs. It did mean that I had decided to be much more open to sharing myself with him sexually.

Δ Δ Δ

Being spiritual does not mean that we have to deny our bodies. Sexuality is a divine gift. It represents the life force that we can celebrate in our relationship with ourself and our mate.

Why was it such a challenge for us to share Sacred Sexuality? Why is shame, guilt, and fear so much easier to access than divine ecstasy? Our childhood programming has instilled belief systems and reaction patterns that resist change. We are creatures of habit, and even pain is often more comfortable than the risk of the unknown. Many people are comfortably miserable in their relationship with their mate. They would rather stay stuck in denial than face their fears.

There are few role models of relationships based on Sacred Sexuality. My hope is that your journey and mine will encourage others to break the bonds of their programming of shame, guilt, and fear. Sacred Sexuality is the final frontier of enlightenment. We are pioneers building models of loving relationships that celebrate the sacredness of sexuality and the sacredness of all life.

PART FOUR

JOURNEY HOME

To love is to return to a home we never left, to remember who we are.

Sam Keen

Chapter 22

Return to Innocence

The gold-yellow of the aspen trees created splashes of brilliance on the Colorado foothills that stretched until they grew into snow-capped peaks. Our drive had taken us through rugged canyons along the Arkansas River. Now we were in the Sangre de Cristo Mountains, approaching the secluded hot springs which was our destination for the day. This was the perfect occasion to go to the springs because we were celebrating the return of Sabrina. She would love the clothing-optional outing.

△ △ △

Five days before the hot springs excursion was the low point in feeling stuck about my sexuality and my sex life with Charlie. I had tried three days of giving him as much sex as he wanted. He liked it — at least he had not complained. I tried to deny my feelings and pretend that I was enjoying our experiment, but I felt frustrated and sad. It seemed that all we were doing was rubbing our bodies together in repetitive Western sex. Of course, there were tender moments, but not the depth of intimacy, not the ecstasy that I craved.

I felt like a dried-up old prune. No matter what we

did, the pleasure was not intense for me like it was for Charlie. His feelings were hurt when I told him about not feeling fulfilled. I had been trying so hard that I had convinced him I was enjoying it. Now his disappointment lay between us like an open chasm. I prayed again for a miracle, for the shift in perception that I had been visualizing for months. I prayed that somehow we would be able to find a way to open our sex life to a more sacred communication of our love.

"What do you really want for our sex life?"

Charlie's question give me the opportunity to articulate what I had yearned for years to experience. "I want a balance between passion and intimacy that we have only experienced in fleeting moments. I want the sacredness of sharing my body and my soul with you that surpasses the physical experience of rubbing bodies together. I want to want you as much as you want me, but in a way that is conscious loving, nothing that feels routine. I love you, Charlie. I want our love life to be a celebration!"

"You don't want much, do you?" he grinned and put his arms around me.

"All I want is to experience ecstasy with you."

"How are you defining ecstasy?"

"It's a state of mind that takes us out of the ordinary. Ecstasy is not transcending our bodies, but perceiving them as temples of the Divine. It's experiencing the divine in each other and all of life. Ecstasy is being one, not just during lovemaking, but more and more of the time. Honey, I really believe that Sacred Sexuality is a doorway to the Divine. In order to enter this doorway we have to have the courage to release our old blueprints, our old programming of guilt and shame about our bodies."

"Aren't you asking for the impossible dream?"

"No. I know it seems like a huge leap to go from ho-hum sex to divine sex, but we don't have to do it all at once."

"Okay, for years we've tried having sex my way. It's time for us to change, to evolve. Where do we start?"

His question surprised me. I had almost given up on his becoming more interested in Tantric loving skills. He had practiced some of the techniques but had shown no lasting interest. We had tried one of the breathing techniques that morning and had not succeeded in completing the exercise. Charlie had gasped for air as I lay on top of him, practicing inverted breathing. That is when one partner inhales, the other exhales. The breathing is done mouth-to-mouth.

"We need to start with the *Yoni* healing exercise." I used the Tantric name for vagina, a term which translates "sacred space."

"When can we do that?"

"I'm not sure ... soon ... I'm scared."

We agreed to wait until I felt ready. Three days passed and we did not make love. Charlie laughingly accused me of giving him a feast or famine. I did not think it was funny. I felt even more scared. What if the healing I had in mind for Yoni did not work? What would we do then? Even more disturbing were my thoughts of what might happen if it did work. Would Sabrina come roaring back into our lives with her insatiable appetite for more than one lover?

In preparation for the healing exercise, I decided to attempt to reintegrate Sabrina into my life. Taking my writing notebook along, I hiked to the top of the hillside above our campground to a place we called Eagle Ridge. On the way I saw a golden eagle circling high above the cliffs that were my destination. It was a beautiful sign. The eagle represents the energy of the East, the sunrise, the opening to a new day. What I was seeking was an opening into a new dimension of my Sacred Sexuality.

I sat on a large rock, facing the East. I quieted my mind to a meditative state. Then I began to write a dialogue in my notebook. I used my right hand to represent my conscious self and my left hand to represent Sabrina. This process of writing, alternating between the dominant and nondominant hands, allows the words to flow easily out of the subconscious mind. My dialogue began simply. "Okay, Sabrina, we need to talk."

The response came quickly after I switched my pen to my left hand. "Yes, we have needed to talk for a long time. I am a very dear part of you that you must stop fearing. I am not your enemy."

"Sabrina, what is your intent?"

"My intent is to be sexually alive and vibrant."

"I can live with that. What are your needs?"

"I need to experience passion, the passion that has been missing from your sex life, to love and be loved in creative ways that keep me excited and fulfilled."

"That's still okay, in fact more than okay. I would like all those things, but what scares me is that you were never satisfied with one man before. I banished you from my life because I was afraid that your addiction to sex would destroy my relationship with my soulmate. My intent is to integrate your lusty passion into my expression of sexuality with my beloved. My needs are to be able to share both passion and intimacy with Charlie in a way that is sacred. Can you agree to that, Sabrina?"

"Yes. I'm excited by the creativity of Sacred Sexuality and the unlimited opportunity to experience ecstasy. I believe it's possible to have passionate, loving sex and intimacy in a monogamous relationship. It must be a flow of energy, a dance. You've been making sex into hard work, rather than enjoying it as a celebration of life. You must take responsibility for your own sexual ecstasy. Then you will be able to fully enjoy sharing ecstasy with Charlie. I think you're going to enjoy having me back."

Putting down my notebook, I closed my eyes and held out my arms. I symbolically embraced this aspect of myself that I had banished for seven years. "You've evolved since we were last together, Sabrina. Welcome back," I whispered.

I placed one hand on Yoni and one hand on my heart, touching the energy centers for passion and intimacy. I breathed deeply, pulling each breath up as though it were coming in through my genitals and feeling it rise into the area of my heart. Then I exhaled, imagining the breath going out of my body through my genitals. I slipped my hand inside my jeans and began caressing Yoni. My sacred space was opening to my touch and felt warm and moist. I understood my craving for balance between passion and intimacy. Sabrina had been passionate for the sake of passion. In order to avoid pain, she had closed her heart to experiencing intimacy. She had made a choice of sex over love, because she did not believe it was possible to have both. When I banished Sabrina, I had banished the passionate, juicy love of sex that I had known only when I was single. I then entered my committed relationship with my soulmate, opening my heart to love, while denying my passion out of fear that I could not be passionate while faithful to one man.

I opened my eyes and again saw the golden eagle high above the ridge. I celebrated my breakthrough with a joyous dance. It was time to go back down the mountain. It was time to heal Yoni.

Δ Δ Δ

Sexual frustrations, the trauma of abuse, and lack of fulfillment are deeply embedded in our pelvic region. This psychological armoring of the body occurs when we deny our pain. These hidden emotions armor the genitals causing a desensitization and a blocking of orgasm. A sacred healing massage of Yoni would help to heal and release this armoring.

I greeted Charlie with a warm hug and whispered, "It's time to heal Yoni. Later I have a surprise for you — for us."

We showered and then climbed into the loft bed of our motor home. We honored each other with the word *Namaste,* which translates, "I salute the God in you." We had decided to incorporate the practice of bowing to each other as a way of beginning our lovemaking by focusing on our sacredness.

Charlie began to massage my body gently, lovingly, with feathery strokes of his hands, focusing his touch on my pelvic area and inner thighs. When I told him that my skin was beginning to tingle, he ran his fingers in a circular motion in my pubic hair. He lightly stimulated my clitoris, using a lubricant, and when I felt ready, he began massaging my Yoni with his finger. I breathed deeply and moved my pelvis as he pressed lightly against the walls of my vagina. Some of the places that he touched triggered sadness and pain, particularly my G spot. I began to cry as he kept his finger pressed against this spot. A kaleidoscope of images of frustrating, unfulfilling sexual encounters moved through my mind.

I allowed my tears to flow as I processed the sadness of having created a protective armoring so that I would not feel threatened by my sexuality. When I was ready, I encouraged Charlie to explore the hidden recesses of my vagina. His loving touch in my deepest places triggered my rage at being raped at fourteen. I sobbed because of the loss of my virginity in such a violent act. I sobbed to release my anger at the religion that had kept me locked in ignorance and had taught me that my body was shameful. I sobbed for innocence lost. I released my sadness for the shattered dreams and sexual frustration in my marriage to Jack. More tears flowed as I released the pain and guilt of my divorce.

Charlie continued his massage as I processed my woundedness from having used my sexuality in an addictive way, for the lack of respect and personal power I had shown in submitting myself to the demeaning experiences of sexual addiction and self-hatred.

Using deep breathing, sound, and movement, I released the woundedness of addiction and abuse. Charlie stayed emotionally present during the entire experience, giving me love and total acceptance. When I felt that my healing was complete, he held me like a mother would hold her child. My breathing returned to normal as Charlie rocked me gently in his arms. He stroked my hair and wiped the tears from my face, whispering, "I love you," over and over.

We did not make love until late that evening. I needed time to process what had occurred during our healing ceremony. I felt a closeness to Charlie that surpassed any previous bonding experience we had shared. I felt my body and my mind returning to the lost innocence of my childhood. For many years I had searched for an experience that would recapture what I had seen the lovers share in my childhood dream. Now ecstasy was within my reach.

Just before midnight I switched off my computer and undressed. Charlie had fallen asleep waiting for me to finish writing my chapter. He smiled sleepily when I climbed the ladder into our loft bed. I nestled close to his naked body and could feel his immediate erection. "What is my surprise?" he asked.

"Sabrina is back," I whispered.

We massaged each other with a fragrant oil. Then Charlie began using his tongue and fingers to bring Yoni to orgasm. I felt an intense orgasmic release when he gently caressed my G spot. Then I began stroking and licking his penis which we call *Lingham.* This Tantric word translates "wand of light." I guided his Lingham into my Yoni. If a woman always inserts Lingham herself, the act of penetration will not trigger memories of rape or abuse. I could tell that he was reaching the point of no return. Just before he would have ejaculated, he took a deep breath, and his body trembled with an implosive orgasm. There was no ejaculatory fluid released, but the body/mind sensations of orgasm were similar. One of the complaints I had expressed to him was that when he would ejaculate, sex would be over, and he would fall asleep. It was as though he would go instead of come. Now he was ready for more pleasure. I felt our passion and intimacy intensify as we made love in different positions, sharing orgasm after orgasm. At times I forgot which body was mine as we soared on wave upon wave of bliss, sharing the oneness that I had dreamed of.

The next morning we made love again, with Charlie still not ejaculating. Then we packed our lunch and drove through breathtaking mountain scenery to the hot springs. Neither of us had experienced a clothing-optional environment. We were ready to experience our nakedness in a healing atmosphere and release our old programming about our bodies.

The drive provided us time to discuss our relationship and the miracle shift in perception that was occurring. I described my reintegration of Sabrina and how it felt to want to make love all the time again, a feeling that I had not had since our courtship. I also told him how happy I was to no longer have an agenda when we had sex. I had felt resentful of his always needing to ejaculate, yet until I began studying Sacred Sexuality, I had believed that our lovemaking was incomplete unless he had finished.

Charlie described our miracle lovemaking as a sharing rather than an act that he did to me. He agreed that there was a creative partnership in our loving that he had never experienced before. At first, he had been hesitant to try the technique of delayed ejaculation which I had suggested. Charlie's first reaction was that it was not manly or that it would cause testicle pain to suppress his ejaculation. But he was open to practicing the exercises that taught him how to control his release of seminal fluid. He explained that he was surprised that he did not feel he was giving up anything. Instead, he was experiencing intense pleasure from his implosive orgasms.

After a three-hour drive, we arrived at the hot springs, prepared to open ourselves to a new experience. We hiked up the trail to the top pool, passing several pools with naked bathers. The pool next to the top had a couple in the shallow water who looked as though they had been making love. They held each other unashamedly while they waved hello. I wanted to be that uninhibited.

The top pool had three people, two men and a woman who were getting ready to leave. The men had on tee shirts and hiking boots. The woman was fully dressed except for being barefoot. She began putting on her hiking boots painfully slowly, giving us ample time to take off our clothes. It seemed as though we were caught in a slow-motion time warp. As I leaned over to place our towels and tote bag on a rock, I was eye level with hairy balls and a dangling penis. I felt embarrassed as I fumbled with the towels. It was only a few seconds which seemed interminable. Then I pulled off my tee shirt, boots, socks, and finally, jeans and panties. I did not look to see if Charlie was matching my pace. Just as I stepped into the pool, I heard one of the men say, "Enjoy your soak," and they were gone.

We had the pool to ourselves for two hours. The sunlight danced on the water, sending shimmering ripples of white-gold light onto our naked bodies. We played and caressed and made love in our private mountain paradise. A warm waterfall cascaded from our pool into the pool below. Yellow and purple wildflowers seemed to smile at us and at their reflection in the water. I made love to my beloved with childlike delight. We continued our play until we heard voices nearby. A couple came into view, wearing only their hiking boots. We invited them to enjoy the pool with us, staying long enough to get comfortable with their presence. Then we got out of the pool and hiked down the hill, carrying our clothes and our lunch. We had forgotten about being hungry.

We stopped for a picnic and discussed our feelings about being in an environment where nudity was the norm. After my initial embarrassment, I loved it. I experienced my body as completely free of inhibition. My senses were alive with the warmth of the sun, the play of the wind against my skin, the tickling sensation of the tiny bubbles in the pool, and the spectacular vista of snow-capped mountains playing tag with the clouds. I felt a oneness, an ecstasy in being a part of the joyous dance of life. Charlie expressed his relief at being free at last from the Southern Baptist programming of his childhood. He had shed his shame, guilt, and fear when he had shed his clothing at the upper pool.

After our lunch we visited a larger pool with half a dozen people soaking in it. We got into the water, and I noticed that Charlie's nose needed more sun screen. I got out of the pool, and leaned over from the waist, searching for the sun screen in my bag. When I got back in the water, Charlie whispered that I had mooned the group. We laughed about my unself-conscious behavior. It no longer mattered if people stared at me. I felt okay about my nakedness.

The rest of the afternoon we enjoyed other pools and sat in the sauna. When we prepared to leave, I felt resistant to putting on my clothes. We had spent an idyllic day in a place of free spirits and unashamed natural beauty of the surroundings and of the human body. I resented having to dress to reenter the real world.

What if the naturalness of the human body and of our sexuality were the true reality? What if the blueprints that have conditioned us to feel shameful and guilty could be released, and we could return to our childlike innocence? I know it is possible to regain paradise. It happened for us through a series of events that threatened to either destroy or heal our relationship. Charlie and I were able to weather the stormy days in which we examined our sex life. I had faith that we could co-create the miracle love that we both wanted and deserved. We undertook a journey that led us into a return to passion and intimacy, and a return to innocence through our acceptance of the sanctity of our bodies.

Δ Δ Δ

Each of us needs to experience a return to innocence, the innocence that we had as babies before the process of negative conditioning and abuse began to cloud our perception of ourselves as sacred, sexual beings. Babies will naturally explore their bodies, delighting in the pleasurable sensations without inhibitions. They have to be taught not to touch their genitals. Through observation of the behavior of adults, children are programmed to deny their bodies. Because of their shame, guilt, and fear programming, children become blindly obedient to beliefs that will rob them of their innocence and their memory that they are divine beings with the sacred gift of a human body.

Banned from paradise by accepting the teachings of original sin, we reenact the myth of Adam and Eve by having to clothe ourselves to hide our shame. Granted, there are climates in which clothing is a protection from the cold, but in general, we hide our beliefs about our bodies in our clothing. What kind of society has made it illegal to be unclothed, and has made the reproductive organs into objects of shame, lust, and abuse? We have become a sexually diseased society, both physically and psychologically. Sexuality is exploited and abused to the extent that over seven billion dollars is spent annually on pornography in the United States!

When we can accept our nakedness as we did as infants, we begin to live fully in our bodies. Our relationship with the entire world changes when we replace shame with pride, guilt with innocence, and fear with courage. We open ourselves to experience our oneness with all life, to experience ecstasy. The separation between our physical and spiritual selves must be healed by resacralizing our bodies, by returning to our lost innocence.

Δ Δ Δ

Nudity is a subject that embarrasses many enlightened people. It presses fear buttons when I ask a group of seminar attendees how they would feel about continuing the training without their clothing. Besides the childhood religious programming about the human body, there is the aspect of self-consciousness about being overweight, out of shape, or otherwise different from the norm of physical perfection portrayed in fashion magazines. Our reaction patterns must be released in order to celebrate our bodies without inhibitions.

Perhaps you can begin by being naked in the privacy of your home. If that is already comfortable for you, go to a place where you can be alone in nature and remove your clothing. Although you do not have to become a card-carrying nudist, you may want to visit a nudist campground or a clothing-optional hot springs or beach. You will be surprised how quickly you will adapt to the totally accepting environment of people whose lifestyle involves social nudism. You will see few perfect bodies. Most nudists have the same problems with weight or bulges that the rest of society has. What you will find is a group of well-adjusted, rugged individualists who respect the privacy of others. People who are comfortable with their nakedness have nothing to hide.

During our travels we became friends with a couple named Alice and Jim. We discussed our feelings about nudity, and Charlie and I shared our experiences in overcoming negative programming about our bodies. Our friends expressed an interest in releasing their fears about nudity but did not feel that they were ready to experience a nudist environment. Recently Alice called me to proudly relate that she and Jim had spent a weekend at a nudist resort. She said that at first she had felt paranoid about going outside their room without her clothes. Jim told her he was there to confront his issues. She agreed, and within five minutes they were strolling around the resort dressed in sandals and sunglasses. Alice said she was amazed at how quickly they both broke through their shame, guilt, and fear programming and were able to experience a miracle shift in perception. They were planning a return trip soon.

Facing our fears about nudity is a shame-buster. Nudity is perfectly natural. Unfortunately, because of our Puritan ethic, it must be practiced in a protected environment. It is our culture which is sick. If these statements disturb you, examine your resistance. What negative programming is hidden in your clothing?

Chapter 23

Sacred Mountain

As I was walking down the mountain trail with Charlie, I looked back at Eagle Ridge, towering overhead. "I'm afraid of spending the night by myself in nature." I heard myself speaking my fear aloud.

"What are you afraid of?" Charlie responded.

"Oh, I don't know, maybe bears and cougars for starters."

"Marina, there are lots of bears and cougars in this area. I suggest that you not spend the night alone in the mountains. Your fear could draw something fearful to you."

"But I only do the things that scare me."

That conversation began my preparation to spend a night alone on Eagle Ridge. I wanted to undertake a vision quest that would give me a message for the journey of Sacred Sexuality, but my logical brain told me it might not be safe. I asked Michelle, who lives nearby in the canyon, "Have you seen any cougars around here lately?"

"Oh, not in the last two or three weeks."

That really comforted me! Then I asked another local person about bears and cougars seen in the campground where we were staying. "We don't get them down here very often, not in the last few weeks, at least. They pretty much stay up on the high ridges." She pointed toward Eagle Ridge, and I shivered in the warm, August sunlight.

I packed my supplies. I would take only water. Fasting is important when seeking a vision, and food would be a magnet for hungry animals. A sleeping bag was a must, but I would sleep under the stars without the protection of a tent. I packed corn meal and Native American tobacco for a ceremony, my flute and drum, and a rain poncho, warm sweatshirt, and gloves.

Then I waited for full moon and clear skies. The night before full moon was misty and cold. Maybe I would not be able to undertake the journey after all. It would be easy to allow the weather to keep me from facing my fears. I was nervous and excited. I had always been envious of people who were fearless, especially in nature, yet it seemed odd that I should be afraid. I loved Mother Earth and her creatures. Why should they frighten me? The unknown lay lurking in the shadows beyond the safety of my warm, dry motor home we call the Starship. No one could hear me on Eagle Ridge if I were in danger. I would be completely alone.

The day of my vision quest brought dark storm clouds from the West, shrouding Eagle Ridge in thunderheads. Then, an hour later the wind blew the storm over the plains, and I was certain it was time to leave. I checked my supplies carefully: two lighters, in case one failed, pine pitch to help start a fire, and drinking water. I was ready. I said good-bye to Charlie and my cat, Jopie, who was sunning lazily on the picnic table. I envied his comfort and safety. I only do the things that scare me, I repeated to myself as I began the hike to Eagle Ridge.

On the way I picked some sage, being careful to leave the main plant intact. That way it would grow back. I sprinkled some tobacco at the base of the plant as an offering of thanksgiving for its gift. Continuing

184

my hike, I braided the sage into a wreath and placed it on my head. The distinctive aroma of this herb, sacred to Native Americans, would be an ally on my quest. The path became steeper, and I questioned why I had added the thermal undershirt and wool vest to my pack. Yet the wind was cool, and warm clothing would be important on the ridge.

When the trail ended, I began my climb up the cliff, thankful for my hiking boots. Grasping rocks and scrub oak branches, I made my way carefully to the place I had chosen for my adventure, Eagle Ridge. The sun would soon be behind the mountains, so I took advantage of the warmth to prepare my site. I placed a stone in each of the four directions and then made a large circle of cornmeal. I spread my sleeping bag inside the circle and dug a small fire pit. After I had gathered dead branches and twigs, there was nothing left to prepare, no dinner to fix. My stomach growled noisily. I had been fasting for three days, waiting for the right time for my journey. A drink of water would have to be dinner.

I climbed part way down the western side of the ridge to watch the sun sink behind the mountains. The rays were warm and comforting. I took off my tee shirt, allowing the golden warmth to caress my breasts. It felt good to be naked in nature. I remembered a time the summer before when I had hiked a Colorado canyon with my friend, Sierra. Our clothes got soaked when we crossed a creek, so we took them off and hiked naked. Being naked in nature returned me to the childlike innocence of the beauty and naturalness of the human body.

My meditative state was interrupted by a sound coming from the scrub oaks behind me. I turned, feeling no fear, and saw something moving behind a rock. I waited, breathing deeply, as the something peered at me. It was a wild turkey. Then I saw five turkeys moving cautiously and looking nervous as they tiptoed past me. I walked to where they had been standing and found a beautiful gift. One of them had dropped a downy soft feather, its green-black tip edged with iridescence. The turkey symbolizes the give-away, the selfless giving of oneself in service. This gift was a powerful way to begin my quest.

The sun dropped reluctantly from view, and immediately the chill of the mountain air invaded my nakedness. I layered warm clothing, thankful for my caution as the wind began to blow harder. There was time before dark to prepare my ceremony for releasing fear. I took small squares of cotton cloth out of my pack. There were two colors, black and red. These squares, called tobacco ties by Native Americans, would hold my prayers for release of fear and for protection. I took a pinch of ceremonial tobacco from a leather pouch. Then I held the tobacco under my nostrils, speaking aloud, "Into this tobacco I breathe my fear of the unknown." I placed the tobacco on a small black square of cloth and tied the square with a piece of string. I made a tobacco tie for each of my fears — cougars and bears, fear of death, fear of storms, and my list continued until I had accessed all my fears. There was soon a pile of tiny bags in front of me. Then I began making the red tobacco ties into which I breathed my prayers for protection. I repeated the same procedure, only I made two of each of my red bags, one to burn and one to keep as a reminder of my prayers.

It would be getting dark soon. I prepared my fire, placing the tobacco ties next to the fire pit. Then I played my drum and chanted, "Where I stand is holy, holy is the ground; forest, mountain, river, listen to my sound; Great Spirit circling all around me." It felt good to play my drum and know that my chant was carried by the wind to the mountains surrounding me. I felt excited and unafraid. I was beginning my act of power.

The darkness gathered around me with the rustle of the wind in the pines. I leaned against a large rock and allowed the darkness to discover that I was unafraid. I got up and danced around my circle, chanting and waving my arms. It felt good to be in this place alone.

I burned my fingers with the lighter as I searched in my pack for the pitch to use for a fire starter. Tiny flames began to lick at the twigs, finally beginning to burn brightly. I placed my tobacco ties one by one into the flames, watching them disappear in the tiny inferno. I had coaxed my fears out of hiding and was facing each of them in this ceremony of release.

While I waited for the moon to show herself, I played my flute, five tones over and over, filling the darkness with the sound of harmony. I watched the moon appear, sending silvery shadows across the canyon. It was so bright that the stars were almost hidden from view.

I contemplated the symbolism of the bear and the cougar. Native Americans revere bear medicine for its power of introspection. The bear's hibernation is a metaphor for our going within the quietness of our intuitive knowing to find the answers to our questions. Cat medicine represents power and courage. It also represents the Sacred Feminine in many Eastern teachings.

Preparing to enter the silence of my inner knowing, I prayerfully requested a vision. I asked that I be given a message that would empower the Sacred Feminine within me and within others to speak our truth with courage. I leaned against the rock, playing again the sound of harmony on my flute, the five tones that would prepare me to receive my vision.

I remained in a meditative state for hours, placing more branches on my fire when it began to die out. In the glow of my tiny fire, perched high on Eagle Ridge, I surrendered myself to whatever vision would find me. Sometime during the night, I slipped into Dreamtime and received the following vision:

It was dawn, and the air was suddenly pierced by

the shrill screeching of a hawk. I looked up to see it flying from the mountains toward the East. As soon as the hawk disappeared, I was startled by the presence of an enormous great-horned owl who was pregnant. She flew overhead, carrying a small green snake in her mouth.

My fire had gone out when I returned to conscious awareness, awakened by the hooting of an owl nearby. My dream vision remained clearly etched in my memory. Its message contains empowering information for our sacred journey. The hawk represents the messenger from the spirit world, flying from the West toward the East, which symbolizes the opening, a new beginning. Hawk's piercing scream represents the persistence with which we must speak our truth about the sacredness of sexuality. The owl brought a transformative message. It represents wisdom and discernment. To many native people it also represents death. I understood it as a symbolic representation of the death of the toxic beliefs of shame, guilt, and fear that have impoverished our experience of sexuality. A dream symbol of a pregnant owl carrying a live snake represents wisdom giving birth to transformation. The green color of the snake represents new life. Wow! When we fearlessly bring the message of Sacred Sexuality into the light of the new day, we will transform our lives and give birth to a new world that is free from shame, guilt, and fear.

I whispered thank you for my vision as I leaned against the rock, allowing the feeling of trust to permeate my being. The absence of fear had opened my intuitive knowing. I had been entrusted with a vision that would empower and heal those who are ready to experience their Sacred Sexuality. I awaited the dawn as the first signs of red-orange began to light the eastern sky. My night on Eagle Ridge was over. I had come to this sacred mountain requesting a vision, and it had found me. I stood to greet the sun, a woman of power, ready to embrace my mission.

Chapter 24

Riding the Waves of Bliss

It was time to begin our fall lecture tour through the South, and neither of us wanted to leave our Colorado canyon. We said a tearful goodbye to Eagle Ridge on the morning of our departure. We hiked to the top of the ridge and made love to each other and the foothills surrounding us. On our way back to camp Charlie spotted a golden eagle circling the cliffs above us. A part of me will always remain in my rugged canyon, the place where I traveled through my fears to my remembrance of myself as a fully empowered sexual, spiritual woman.

We had been on the road for a week when Charlie said abruptly, "Marina, we need to talk. I'm feeling uncertain about what's going on with our sex life."

"You're right, Sweetheart. I've been feeling the tension between us. You know we've just been on the road a week, and I've felt exhausted from all the packing and running around getting ready for our tour. Wait, that sounds like an excuse as to why I haven't felt like making love."

"I have this uneasy feeling that the bliss we shared in our canyon won't last with the pressures of touring.

What's really going on?"

Charlie's question was one I had been asking myself. The first day we had stopped our motor home at a rest area to make love. It seemed as though we were bringing our bliss with us. We had made love two more times, and I had felt less and less passionate. It had felt as though we were just rubbing bodies together. Something was missing. The last two days I had been ignoring him. "I'm not sure how to explain what I'm feeling. I think I've felt that if we made love it would be servicing you again, and I don't want to access that blueprint."

"What I'd like to know is what to expect in our sexual relationship. Should I expect sex twice a day like in the canyon, or once a day or once or twice a week? I don't want to pressure you, but I was certainly getting used to the steady diet of lovemaking."

Charlie's questions seemed fair. "I would like to feel like making love at least once a day, but I don't have the energy for it right now. I need a few days to figure out what's going on."

"You've got it." There was no longer any resentment in his voice.

We had been using Tantric breathing to bring sexual energy from our pelvic regions up to our brains. Charlie had become a master of the implosive orgasm, able to control his ejaculation and experience multiple orgasms. His most recent experience had taken him into an orgasm that continued to build for several minutes. I had watched him, fascinated by his enjoyment of this new skill, yet strangely dissociated from what was going on. I felt dispassionate, as though I were observing someone else making love. I was envious and was beginning to feel like a dried-up old prune again.

We waited three days and then began making love again daily. I was still feeling disinterested but determined to see that Charlie was satisfied. After one of our lovemaking sessions, I felt tears of disappointment trickling down my cheeks. Charlie said he would rather be celibate than see me cry after making love. I wondered if I was returning to my old blueprints and decided something had to change. We had reached a plateau in our Sacred Sexuality exploration, and I was ready for a deeper experience of oneness.

Tantric techniques seemed to be stalling out for us, so I told Charlie we should put our study aside for a while and just have Western sex. He suggested candlelight, massage, and soft music. I suggested that we forget the trimmings and just get down to the main course — I was thinking we should just get it over with for a few days. I used my frustration to spark the passion that had been missing from my experience. I jumped on top of Charlie after first giving him oral sex. He offered to reciprocate, and I told him that this time was just for his pleasure. He asked if I would please enjoy it, too, or I would be creating more body armoring. I told him to just focus on his pleasure, that I had put aside my pleasure for the moment. In the process of trying to get him to ejaculate, we both became very excited. I rode him furiously, pulling his Lingham with my love muscle, certain that he would ejaculate quickly. He had become so good at ejaculatory control that he was able to withstand the temptation to let go right away. I felt my heart breaking open with love as we held each other tenderly. Then we finished in the missionary position. I joined his cries of pleasure with my own release.

Δ Δ Δ

I realized that I had become obsessed with experiencing ecstasy. I had been ignoring daily opportunities to experience it while I went in search of ecstasy with a capital E! The trouble with ecstasy is that as soon as we think we can grasp and understand it, it disappears under our scrutiny.

As soon as I became aware that I had taken back my blueprint of unworthiness of ecstasy, I felt the old beliefs slipping away like a dead skin that I was shedding. I had prayed for another miracle shift in perception, and I got the message. I had been so focused on Tantric techniques that I had become goal oriented. It was time to return to a more playful attitude. Instead of pushing energy, I committed to allowing the energy to flow more gently. I would continue my Tantric practices in self-pleasuring and would be more of a nurturing, playful partner for my soulmate.

Our tour had brought us to a beautiful section of the Gulf Coast, Gulf Shores, Alabama, where we parked our motor home at a surfside RV park. Our front yard consisted of miles of sun-drenched beaches with sugar-white sand and sparkling green-blue ocean forty feet from our door. The hypnotic rhythm of the waves had a calming effect on my physical, mental, and emotional state.

It was after one of my early morning runs along the beach, feeling radiantly alive and energized, that I experienced a breakthrough in giving myself ecstasy. Charlie was waist deep in the surf, fishing for flounder for lunch. I sat cross-legged on our sofa, attuning my breathing to the rhythm of the ocean. I began rubbing my breasts and then massaged Yoni with a firm, yet gentle touch. When I felt my excitement building, I became completely still, locking my PC and anal muscles. I breathed deeply, drawing the energy upward from my genital region to each of my chakras.

The chakras are seven energy centers that correspond to seven regions of the body — the base of the spine, called the base chakra; the genital area, called the root chakra; the base of the rib cage, called the solar plexus chakra; between the breast bones, called the heart chakra; between the collar bones, called the throat chakra; between the eyebrows, called the third eye chakra; and the top of the head, called the crown chakra. I was experiencing a Tantric practice called Riding the Wild Tiger, which alternates periods of arousal with a deep calm. I focused on feeling and visualizing energy traveling up and down my spine. I practiced sexual breathing, pulling the air up through my genitals to each of the chakra centers in succession, always sending the energy back down the spine and out the genitals. Periodically I would renew my sexual arousal by self-pleasuring.

It was a magical moment when I experienced the sensation of my sexual energy rising up my spine and shooting out the crown chakra. For moments that seemed endless, I felt as though I were floating through the galaxies, my being expanding to become one with the universe. It was a delicious, blissful experience, one of many that followed as I continued to awaken to my capacity for ecstasy. Over time I became comfortable with the practice, confident of my ability to give myself ecstasy.

Then I shared the process with Charlie, and we Rode the Wild Tiger together. We began by bowing to each other and then enjoyed a long hug, breathing in unison for a few minutes. We stimulated each other until we both felt sexually aroused. I lay on top of Charlie with Lingham inside Yoni. We harmonized our breathing while we visualized a warm golden light spiraling from our genitals through each energy center to the top of our heads and then back down to the genital region again. Visualizing the golden light provides a healing bath of energy for all the organs of the body.

We tightened our pelvic muscles, bringing our breath and the golden light up the spine into the chakra centers, imagining ourselves melting into each other. We opened ourselves to energy vibrations, moving our bodies only when necessary to maintain our sexual arousal. The vibrations were barely noticeable at first. As we continued this practice, we began to sense a warmth and a tingling in the chakras as we focused on them. Since I am more visual, it was easier for me to focus on the spiraling light. We continued holding each other after our practice and surrendered to an implosive orgasm. I felt deeply connected to this man who was ready to share ecstasy with me. "I love you, Charlie," I whispered.

Our capacity for shared ecstasy was increasing. We had committed one evening a week to practicing Tantra together, and soon, we were relaxing into the practice on a daily basis. Our deepest ecstasy occurred with the Tantric position called *yab yum,* in which I sat in Charlie's lap facing him, with his Lingham in my Yoni. We would first play with other positions, getting ourselves fully aroused. Just before reaching orgasm, we switched to the *yab yum* position. This position involves minimal outward movement. Instead, the sexual energy is contained by locking the PC and anal muscles, while visualizing a spiraling light moving up the spine and out the crown chakra, then back down and out the genitals. At first we practiced breathing in unison. Then we shifted to inverted breathing, where one of us inhaled while the other exhaled.

We were locked in a tight embrace, our eyes gazing deeply into each other's soul. Suddenly I experienced a mind-blowing sensation. Every cell in my body felt as though it were vibrating. Ripples of pleasure surged up and down my spine. I focused on breathing and relaxed into the full-body orgasm called Riding the Waves of Bliss. I lost all sense of separate self as my body and my soul melted into Charlie. I was floating through inner space on a sacred journey of bliss. I became one with the surging power of the waves crashing on the shore outside our motor home. I entered the stillness of a calm sea and was one with the ripples that stretched into infinity. My awareness expanded until there seemed to be no difference between us. I became Lingham and Charlie was Yoni. All boundaries between us disappeared in this blissful voyage into oneness. This was the ecstasy that I had dreamed of since childhood. We continue to enjoy many sacred practices, although they often lead us to Riding the Waves of Bliss.

△ △ △

My intent is to introduce you to some of the language and practices of Tantra. I hope that my experiences will interest you in exploring the subject more deeply. There are many texts available which offer adaptations of Tantric practices for Western lovers. The most comprehensive and easy-to-follow is *The Art of Sexual Ecstasy* by Margo Anand.

A commitment to share Sacred Sexuality offers many opportunities to develop patience. Open communications are a prerequisite to developing the trust that leads to deeper levels of intimacy. When studying sacred techniques, continue to practice, even if you feel that nothing is happening, trusting the process to work with time and patience. There is a beautiful statement from Huna teachings: "When you think that nothing is happening, then the magic has begun."

A playful attitude lessens goal orientation and helps you stay in the present moment. When I focused on the end result instead of enjoying the journey, I tried to pursue ecstasy instead of savoring the ecstasy in each moment. Life is a series of blissful moments whether I am sharing sex with my beloved or going for a run, talking to a friend or driving my motor home, writing this chapter or playing my flute. When we are one with the sacredness of all life, every moment is sacred.

Chapter 25

Dancing with the Dolphins

"There they are!" Those three words started the adrenalin pumping in my veins. I breathed deeply, trying to remain in an alpha state of awareness. Three, no four, bottle-nosed dolphins had appeared about thirty yards from our boat. Charlie and I were waiting for their next surfacing. We were not disappointed. They were getting closer, close enough for us to hear the exploding sound of their breathing, close enough for us to see the blue-gray iridescence of their bodies slicing through the water. It was time for me to jump out of our rubber boat to join them.

I had been waiting for this moment. Swimming with the dolphins had been my dream for years. I wanted to communicate with them in the wild, to learn truths from them that would apply to the journey of Sacred Sexuality. The year before, we had taken our little rubber boat out into the Gulf of Mexico, and the dolphins had come. I had not been prepared to jump in the water then. Now I was ready.

I tightened the straps on my life vest and pulled down my snorkel mask. Then I took a deep breath and slipped out of the boat into the chilly water. I was grateful for the warmth of my wet suit. It kept me from shivering as I had the week before when I had tried swimming in the surf.

"Dolphins love to play. They're like great big pussy cats," a friend had told me. He had swum with them in the wild. "You just need to call them to you by getting in an altered state and projecting your love to them."

Okay, beautiful dolphins, I thought. Here I am. Let's play. Then I saw them leaving. I tried to swim after them, which of course, was ludicrous. They did a lovely water ballet, dancing through the air with graceful leaps. They seemed to be saying, "We'll be back. Don't be so attached to results, and remember to be patient."

The following day I waited impatiently for the wind to calm down. Another day of stormy seas passed. Finally, we were able to go out, although the sea was still churning. It was cloudy and windy, and there was no sign of our dolphin friends. We waited for thirty minutes and decided to return to shore. Then we heard the sound of their breathing and their splashing in the waves. We headed our boat in their direction, but they were moving quickly and soon disappeared from sight.

The dolphin search was becoming quite an odyssey. I wondered if we were trying too hard, pushing energy, instead of allowing it to flow. I spent time in meditation, asking the dolphins if they had a message for me. The message came, Be patient. Release your goal orientation. Wait and we will come.

Heavy fog rolled in off the water the next morning, a fog that permeated the air with drops of moisture and dripped like rain from the picnic table onto our patio. It was difficult to differentiate between the sea, sky, and sand. They were all the same dreary gray. By midmorning the sun had chased the fog away, and I took my notebook computer outside to keep me company while I scanned the horizon. There was no sign of my friends yet. I committed to spending the morning writing unless I was interrupted by the call of the dolphins.

The sea was like a lake of glass, with miniature waves barely frothing as they broke onto the shore. I continued writing, my computer screen and I shaded by our red and blue umbrella. Hours passed and still no sign of dolphins. I put away my computer and got into my wet suit. Charlie was already in our little boat. This was an odyssey of trust. The dolphins would come when they were ready.

The water was an intense green-blue that seemed miles deep. We watched mullet jumping and jelly fish floating lazily by, their long tentacles trailing gracefully. I began breathing deeply, allowing the gentle rocking of the boat to draw me into an altered state of consciousness. A few minutes later Charlie said the magic words, "There they are!" I continued my deep breathing, sending loving thoughts. These dolphins were in a hurry. They did not stop to play as they sped toward their destination.

"They'll be back." I was certain that we would see them again. We played in the limpid waters, discussing the teaching of the dolphins. "There's a reason why I feel compelled to communicate with these beautiful beings. I believe they have a message for this journey, and I'm prepared to wait as long as it takes."

"Do you think they even care about you?" Charlie responded. He was testing me.

"Honey, are your doubts keeping them away?"

He hesitated before answering. "I don't think so. They've never failed to show up."

A few minutes later they returned, with more dolphins. Now we were surrounded by two groups of them, swimming in circles, closer and closer to our boat. I tightened my life jacket and jumped into the water. Okay, here I am. I'm ready. I continued to breathe deeply as I swam toward the closest fins. They were emitting a harsh, barking sound when they started swimming away. "Come back," I called. Suddenly two dolphins turned around and headed straight toward me. I treaded water and waited, reminding myself to keep breathing. "Come play with me," I called to them, but they veered away.

Two more dolphins headed toward me, I waited a few moments, moments that seemed like hours. Any instant they would be surfacing right beside me, and I was right. One was on either side of me, almost close enough to touch. Don't push energy, I kept repeating to myself. Let them make the first move. Then I felt one of them brushing up against me, and I reached out to touch its dorsal fin. It responded to my touch by raising its head to meet my gaze before disappearing under the water. I entered another time and space, a time of primal innocence as I surrendered myself to the joy of playing with these magical creatures. I stroked their rostrums and their backs and tried to mimic their chatter as they churned through the water. Too soon, they swam away, but our connection will remain in my heart forever.

Dolphins are extremely exuberant creatures, totally uninhibited as they roughhouse with each other in their sensuous play. Because of their openness to human contact, I consider them midwives assisting in the evolution of human consciousness. These highly intelligent beings have much to teach us. They are a powerful reminder of the interconnectedness of all life. They, too, are on a sacred journey, a journey that is woven together with ours through time beyond time.

Communicating with the dolphins has had a profound impact on my journey. Their message is a reminder that we need to breathe deeply and release our attachment to results. The dolphins remind us to play and to be exuberant. Our journey is one of trust and patience as we remember our sacred, sexual selves.

Chapter 26

Charlie's Story

Charlie Oakwind is a unique man. He possesses all the qualities I had dreamed of in a soulmate: loving, gentle, nurturing, creative, playful, and open to growth, as well as confident, powerful, action-oriented, and independent. Added to that are his humor, charm, and overactive sex drive. Charlie is my life partner, my best friend, my editor, and the author of *The ABZ's of High Performance*. He is a talented artist, the creator of Sacred Medicine Tools — native drums, rattles, and flutes. I have asked him to write a chapter briefly outlining his life story, with the emphasis on sexuality. I know you will enjoy both his comments and his writing style.

Δ Δ Δ

Like Marina, I was born in a foreign country — Southern Oklahoma! I was raised by loving parents on a 360 acre, red-dirt farm. Mom and Dad were lukewarm Southern Baptists who saw to it that I was in Sunday School and church an average of one out of two Sundays.

My dad was a man's man without being macho. He let me know that he loved me without words. He took me hunting and fishing as often as he could and never went without me. He could fix anything, which was a must on a working farm. He taught me through example that a man was the head of the household and that the expression of emotions was wimpy. He also taught me to work hard, be honest, not drink to excess, treat people fairly, and enjoy each day to the fullest. I love him beyond words, as do my older brother and sister.

My mother is a unique woman. She was literally purchased by my grandparents from Ora Oakwind, an unmarried Choctaw Indian teenager, for two cows and a horse. The reason my grandparents bought her was because Grandpa was her real father. Mom was a love-child born nine months after my granddad's bachelor party. Grandpa and Ora were childhood sweethearts in an era when white people and Native Americans did not normally marry.

Mom was a little warmer lukewarm Southern Baptist than Dad, at least verbally. Neither of them read the Bible unless under duress, but they did quote moralistic paraphrases as needed in order to raise three well-behaved children.

I never really seemed to fit into my family. I was a loner who was interested in science, art, and creative expression. Farm life demanded that I drive tractors, break horses, milk cows, slop the hogs, gather eggs, and haul hay. I was not a good farm worker like my brother because my heart wasn't in it. Being different made me feel alone, misunderstood, and unworthy.

Now for the juicy part, sex education. There was none! Being raised on a farm did have its advantages. I could watch bulls service cows, roosters top off hens, and dogs get hung up doing it. I noticed that horses had big ones, pigs were awkward, and butterflies and dragonflies made a dance of it. I knew what my wee-wee was for long before it became fully functional. Since we never talked about "it," I had to piece together the sex puzzle slowly, painfully. The silence surrounding human sexuality taught me that sex was sinful, guilt-ridden, and for marriage only.

My first nocturnal emission, called a wet dream in Oklahoma, came as a shock. I thought I was hemorrhaging Elmer's Glue! I soon learned it was a lot more fun to masturbate than to waste my ejaculatory fluid on a wet dream. I felt guilty about self-pleasuring and lived in mortal fear of being caught.

I became interested in girls much earlier than they became interested in me. I had started to school a year early because my mother was the teacher in the one-room, country schoolhouse. I was always the smallest boy in my class. Luckily, I started growing during my sophomore year in high school and was soon one of the tallest boys in my class. I did well in football and basketball and was elected class president during my junior and senior years. That helped my confidence and dating potential immensely.

I would date a girl until I got the impression that she would consider going all the way if I would consider marrying her. I was fearful of getting anyone pregnant, and knew I did not want to follow my brother's lead of marrying young. I did enjoy the hunt, though, and did my share of playing with developing young breasts and smooth white legs. I felt guilty but it was worth it.

Nudity was a big issue for me. I longed to see naked girl bodies in person. I was only successful a few times. It was a thrill to accidentally see our high school homecoming queen, Debbie, changing clothes during a school play rehearsal. Another time a buddy discovered that there was a small hole in the wall of the girls' gym class dressing room where a few of us fellows obtained a week of anatomy training before we were caught by one of the girls' brothers. It was a sad day when the school custodian repaired the hole. I always felt sinful peeking, but again, it was worth it. If a girlfriend allowed me to see her naked, I considered her a slut and would drop her immediately — after a look or two.

I was normal for my region of the country — more interested in being a good Christian than in sexuality. In fact, I considered Christianity and sexuality to be polar opposites. Yet I craved the intimacy and validation which sexual interactions provided.

I survived my high school years and headed for Oklahoma State University on a scholastic scholarship, still a virgin and proud of it. I had been through a born-again experience during my early high school days and was saving myself for marriage. I must admit I was a horny virgin and enjoyed sex games like hugging, kissing, and petting, stopping short of doing "it."

When I was seven years old, I had asked my mom about marriage. She told me that someday when I grew up I would meet the perfect girl for me. She said that I would know it immediately, and that we would get married and have children, living happily ever after. By my senior year of college, I had given up on Mom's idealistic prediction and had started looking for a wife. It was an unwritten law of campus life that you found your spouse while attending college. It would have been embarrassing to leave college as a bachelor. I was also worried about being drafted into the army and being killed before I had done "it" even once. I married the first nice girl that said yes. It was a marriage destined for divorce from the moment the Methodist preacher said, "I pronounce you man and wife."

My marriage was a twenty-year study in religious abuse. We were both unhappy with each other. She had married me to also avoid the unmarried college graduate syndrome. We perfected marital sarcasm to a fine art. We tortured each other for twenty years, and during that time raised two natural and two adopted children. I developed outside hobbies to entertain myself. I coached my sons' Little League football and basketball teams, and went fishing, hiking, and camping as often as possible. I also began an avocation that would eventually become my vocation, instructing adult self-improvement classes. I was never unfaithful to my wedding vows because that would have been a sin. No Oakwind had ever gotten a divorce, and I did not want to be the first. I felt cheated, disappointed, and a profound sense of loneliness. Life just wasn't fair.

Our sex life was poor, if not worse than awful. She did not seem to be interested in sex except for bimonthly servicing to meet her commitment to love, honor, and obey. I found my masturbation abilities to be of great value in maintaining my sanity, although I felt cheated. I believed a wife should be a "bought-and-paid-for" sex partner. My sexual advances were usually met with minor medical emergencies such as headaches, upset stomach, and accusations of my being oversexed. I felt trapped by the institution of marriage and the religious dogma that used guilt and fear to perpetuate my pain. It was not a marriage made in heaven, but it did give me insight into hell.

When I look back at this time, I see myself as an untalented lover married to a disinterested wife without enough love to continue the relationship. If it had not been for our religious beliefs and social norms, our marriage would not have lasted a year. I wish her well and hope that someday we can both laugh about our twenty-year experience in marital prison camp.

After my separation I was lost in a sea of despair, guilt, shame, and loneliness. I missed my children and even missed the comfort of my self-imposed prison. I briefly returned to my marriage because of my loneliness and because a Baptist preacher friend of mine told me I had no Biblical justification for divorce. Nothing had changed, so after six months I again filed for divorce.

This time I drowned my pain in my work and sexual excesses. Often I would cry like a baby after having sex with a woman I didn't love. I felt guilty of premeditated fornication. That feeling would pass as seminal buildup would build up. For two years I played the game of sex with much success, if you consider sports sex a game. Finally, out of disgust and desperation, I decided to hang up my condoms and retire. I quit chasing women and started working on discovering who Charlie Oakwind really was and if he was worth salvaging. I started attending a new church, a liberal Christian church that stressed that God was not a mean old man on a cloud somewhere up in the sky, but a universal power or spirit, a God/Goddess, a Father/Mother God. I discovered that I was not a guilty sinner. The spirit of God dwelled in Charlie. I was okay.

Then I read Richard Bach's *Bridge Across Forever*. Mom was right! There was a perfect woman out there somewhere sent to earth to be my soulmate. Wow! Where was she? I looked into the eyes of women in my age range, searching for a soul connection. Occasionally, I would tire of looking and succumb to an evening of physical pleasure with another lonely spirit sister. I even felt guilty because I felt as though I were not being true to my soulmate.

When I first saw Marina Raye I was unimpressed, not because she was too beautiful to be interested in me, but because she was too young. I wanted a mature soulmate who had raised her family, who was ready to enjoy life, and enjoy me.

I was around Marina several times before I found out that she was older than her beautiful face and figure communicated. I had a very real rush of anticipation as I approached her at a business meeting break in Tulsa. The moment our eyes met, really met, I knew that she was my soulmate. Logic told me that I was a dreamer, but my essence told me that my search was over — I was home.

Although I was confident that Marina recognized

me as her beloved, I knew that her logical thinking would have to get accustomed to the idea. I felt euphoric and decided immediately that in order for our relationship to last, I must know beyond uncertainty that Marina and I were soulmates. I would not allow anything or anyone to come between us. "Beyond uncertainty" was challenged immediately. Marina is a very honest person and insisted on telling me about her sexual past. I had suspected that she was no saint, but her past was a bit much for me to accept all at once. I felt like a sexual rookie thrust into the big leagues. Beyond uncertainty assured me that in order for Marina and me to meet, we had to have lived our lives exactly the way we had lived them. We had been headed toward each other on our divine paths from the moment of our conception. We were soulmates.

Soulmates raised in the Western culture of the twentieth century are destined for patriarchal sex, a man's sport that requires a woman for its playing field. Although I had experienced sex with women who enjoyed their limited role as ejaculation receptacles for horny penises, Marina was exceptional. She took sex to a new level of excitement, to an art form. She was the best lover I had ever had, especially since I was so very much in love with her. Not only was she warm, loving, eager, and enthusiastic in bed, but she was a truly remarkable person. She was an accomplished musician, writer, professional speaker, trainer, environmentalist, metaphysician, world traveler, and spiritual teacher. She was perfect, and she was my soulmate.

When I found out she had been unfaithful to me by spending the week after our Colorado vacation with Ray, I felt crushed, betrayed, and angry. I wanted to run, but how do you run away from your soulmate? I had to ask myself which was more important, my pride or my happiness. Was I being liberal and understanding, or was I being a wimpy, pussy-whipped, henpecked, spineless jellyfish? My internal dialogue did get a bit carried away.

Marina assured me that her moment of weakness should not interfere with our lifetime of bliss. Her words of assurance and her making-up ritual convinced me that a soulmate relationship leads to maximum challenge, growth, and ecstasy.

Strange things happen in relationships of long duration. Even soulmate relationships fall prey to routines and schedules. As months became years, I started feeling as though our sex life had slipped from the best possible to extremely average. Since it was better than anything I had ever experienced in my marriage, I did not complain — much. I did indulge in a little sarcasm here and there, a bit of dramatic self-pity at the end of a long day, secretly yearning for the good old, sexy dating days. It often worked!

We would rekindle the passion of those good old days with some candlelight, massage, mood music, and slow, tender holding followed by hard and fast pumping. Ejaculation would make a new man of me. My happy genes seemed to be in my jeans.

Finally, due to Marina's insatiable appetite for knowledge and enlightenment, she discovered Sacred Sexuality. Nothing has brought me more spiritual or sexual satisfaction than the path of Sacred Sexuality. Like most Western men, I fought it as though change were threatening my very survival. I didn't want to change my sexual habits. I just wanted more of what I wasn't getting enough of.

The first thing I had to eliminate was goal orientation in our lovemaking. This meant that I did not ejaculate every time we made love. My first thoughts were negative. I did not want to have testicle pain. I did not want to fight the old premature ejaculation thing again. I did not want to give up the euphoria of the nine seconds of ejaculatory orgasm. The only reason I agreed to try this different way of making love was that I knew it would mean experimentation, which would mean more sex — what a great research project! I also love Marina very much and am generally willing to do whatever makes her happy.

The research quickly became a way of life. Through practice I learned ejaculatory control by strengthening my PC muscles. I did fifty to one hundred contractions a day until I could feel the strength developing. I still do thirty to fifty a day to maintain my PC muscle strength. When we are making love, I control my ejaculation by stopping all movement and immediately holding my breath for ten seconds. Then I do ten PC muscle contractions while pressing my tongue against the roof of my mouth.

The most enjoyable aspect of this non-goal orientation is that you do not have to give up orgasms. You simply separate orgasm from ejaculation. You can have as many implosive orgasms as you like and for as long as you like. You start by faking it. Remember a time when you had a great orgasm. You held your breath, tightened your anal and PC muscles, you moaned in ecstasy, and closed your eyes so tight you had wrinkles from ear to ear. Energy exploded out the top of your head like a geyser while you sprayed your hot semen into your lover's hungry vagina. All you have to do is recreate those feelings exactly, only without the ejaculation. It helps to get close to an ejaculatory feeling, but not so close as to lose control.

Other aspects that are revolutionary about non-goal orientation are the absence of performance anxiety, the nurturing and bonding of leisurely sex play, the energy flow and buildup as opposed to the post-ejaculatory loss of energy, the added hours of expressing love, and the sacred high of meditation added to the sacred high of sexual stimulation.

Just so you won't think I am totally non-goal oriented, I do have a wonderful ejaculatory orgasm about every fourth or fifth time we make love. We now make love on a daily basis, or at least an average of once a day. This is not a rule set in stone. If we have a day that does not lend itself to sex play, then that is okay, too. If two or three times a day is appropriate, then we go for it. We don't make rules — it violates the non-goal orientation.

Δ Δ Δ

Marina has always been very open in her communication with me. I always know how she is feeling about our relationship. This is fairly common among women and is epitomized by the stereotype of the emotional, talkative woman.

I have been more reserved with my feelings. If I did feel strongly about a relationship issue, I knew it would probably pass within a day or two, so I just kept my mouth shut. I stuffed my emotions, which usually showed by my being a grump. I lived up to the stereotype of the strong, silent man.

To correct my heavy-duty, male programming, I had to analyze my woundedness to find its sacred gifts. When I looked for my greatest woundedness, it was obvious. My obedience to fundamentalist religion had caused me to lose my identity, my soul, to the predictable path. I was so unhappy in my first marriage that I had to deny my emotions and hide behind the masculine mask of strength and confidence. I'll never forget the rainy day in 1981, when I started crying in the middle of isle #8 of the local Safeway grocery store. I thought I was having a nervous breakdown. Maybe I was. It didn't take me long to figure out that I had two choices — the funny farm or my freedom to be me. I could no longer be the projection of Mr. Middle Class American Male. My inability to express my emotions and get my needs met almost destroyed my life. Instead, it was the turning point that has allowed me to embrace my feelings and express them as a whole, complete being.

The greatest challenge to men is to be present with their emotions. The men who attend our Sacred Sexuality Workshops often begin the weekend by intellectualizing their woundedness, thus repeating their reaction patterns of shame, guilt, and fear. I urge my brothers to do whatever is necessary to open themselves to their deepest emotions and express them unashamedly. We must be willing to release our bulldog grip on left-brain logic. We must welcome the balance of our Inner Soulmate. We must be willing to be whole.

Δ Δ Δ

The biggest victory in my life has been ridding myself of shame, guilt, and fear programming. I feel very fortunate to have found both Great Spirit and Marina Raye. I'm a lucky guy!

PART FIVE

JOURNEY FROM SCARED TO SACRED SEXUALITY

Sacred sex, which is the experience of ecstasy, is the real sexual revolution.

Georg Feuerstein, *Sacred Sexuality*

Chapter 27

Normalizing Sacred Sexuality

"**I**'m scared of sacred sexuality," the man who introduced himself as John said. "Last night I was talking to a woman with whom I've had a sexual relationship in the past. We're just friends now. I tried to express to her my fear of the sacredness of sex, and she didn't seem to understand me at all. I've only experienced what I consider a sacred encounter with another human being, either sexually or nonsexually, a few times in my life."

I asked John what he was afraid of. "Oh ... having a real encounter is so very rare. Maybe what's scary is to really connect with someone by looking into their soul. It makes me feel vulnerable, totally exposed. It's like I'm looking into the eyes of God in that fleeting moment. Then I wonder if this God-person really sees into my soul, really knows my essence, will they still like me. I'm afraid they'll judge me for being petty or arrogant, inept or foolish."

I commended John for his vulnerability in expressing his fears. He mentioned that he was on a spiritual path. He felt that he was growing, but it was an awkward time. I wished I could have recommended a magic pill to alleviate his fears. I wanted to tell him that he was choosing to stay stuck in his fears instead of releasing them, but that was too simplistic. John must find the gift in his fear on his own journey. Fear can be our sacred teacher if we confront it and work our way through it.

One of the organizations that sponsored my Sacred Sexuality Workshop advertised in their newsletter that I would be presenting a workshop on "Scared" Sexuality. It was amusing, yet a profound Freudian slip of someone's word processor. To most of us sexuality has been scary far more often than sacred!

How can we normalize sexuality, taking it from scared to sacred? We undertake an individual journey into our soul, the heroic journey referred to by mythologist, Joseph Campbell. This journey leads us to explore the fearful places where our shadow dwells, the places that we have denied for most of our lives. Acknowledging our fears and healing the shame from our past negative conditioning is the first step on this journey.

We need to be reassured that we can make it to the other side of our fears. A single father, recently divorced, called to register for a seminar. He said, "You have no idea how scared I am of my sexuality. I waited until the last minute because I didn't think I could pick up the phone to dial your number. I'm terrified. I think I've lived in denial all of my life."

It takes courage to express our emotions and our fears. Until we acknowledge these emotions, we will remain stuck. Many women are speaking freely about their fears, sharing them to empower themselves and others. Because of societal conditioning, it is an even bigger leap for men to speak out. I applaud the men who are facing their woundedness and walking through their fears. The men's movement is helping my brothers to liberate their hearts. As they share their stories, chant, drum, dance, laugh, and cry together, they open themselves to fully experience their emotions, release their fears, and embrace their wholeness.

A man named Steve was describing his feelings of stuckness. "I feel like I've been comatose all my life. I know I need to change, but I'm afraid."

After acknowledging his feelings, my response to Steve was, "If you don't change, you will be a victim of your own history."

Much of our sexual history has been heavily influenced by the teachings of the salvation psychology of fundamentalist religions. We are told that we must be saved from ourselves. Our natural state is described as sinful, evil, and separate from God.

One of the saddest comments came from a woman at one of my booksignings in Huntington Beach, California. While she was looking at my book, *Do You Have an Owner's Manual for Your Brain?*, I mentioned that it was self-help/psychology in fiction form. "Oh, I'm a Christian," she responded as she dropped my book on the table. "I know better than to get involved in 'self' anything!" As long as we disempower ourselves with these beliefs, we will experience shame, guilt, and fear. Fortunately, many of us have released these toxic beliefs and are healing the woundedness caused by religious abuse.

In my workshops, participants sometimes tell gender-biased jokes as a method of diffusing their embarrassment about their sexuality. Laughter often covers up our pain. I ask the group, "What are we perpetuating by joining this laughter?" Refuse to give passive approval to any conversation or experience that dishonors the sacredness of sexuality. Tell people why you are turned off by their jokes or negative sexual comments.

As we move through our fears, we release the myth that we are separate from the creative force of life. A vital aspect of normalizing Sacred Sexuality is desensitizing ourselves to nudity. As long as we are ashamed of our bodies, we will block our experience of ecstasy. One of the most destructive effects of fundamentalist religions is body-negative programming. Although we may no longer believe that our bodies are shameful, many of us still have reaction patterns firmly in place that keep us stuck in shame and fear about our bodies.

A woman related that even though she knew better, she still felt that her genitals were shameful. She had been programmed with hand-me-down shame by her mother, who was taught by her mother, who was taught by her mother ... We will expand our understanding of Sacred Sexuality as we lovingly accept our bodies and release our shame programming about our nakedness. Our clothing is a place where we can hide our shame and guilt. A man at a nudist resort was joking about people who refuse to accept nudity as a natural state. He called them "textile types," and laughingly stated, "If God had meant for us to be naked, we would have been born that way!"

Δ Δ Δ

Normalizing Sacred Sexuality involves seeing the Divine in everything. We have been conditioned to think of the sacred as something that is set apart, separate from our daily lives. We have confined sex to the bedroom and sacredness to the church, cathedral, or temple. A hopeful sign of the shift in consciousness is that many churches are willing to sponsor my workshops. Unfortunately, some individuals feel that they are too spiritual to have anything to do with the body. This attitude represents as much denial as fundamentalist religion. It is still body-negative programming. What better place to normalize Sacred Sexuality than in a church sanctuary! As parents receive training in Sacred Sexuality, they will teach their children in ways that will stop the cycle of abuse. I believe that children who are taught to respect the sanctity of their bodies will have a strong self-image and be better protected from sexual abuse.

By acknowledging the divine within us we recognize the divine in others, in all of life. I asked a friend who had recently returned from India what her most profound teaching was. She said that it was the question which her guru had asked her, "Well, Barbara, have you gotten it yet?"

"Got what?"

"The simplicity of it all, that everything is God. The chair upon which you are sitting, my robe, the pitcher of water, the floor, the fly that buzzes around our heads, it's all God! There is no need to complicate your life with searching for God. It is here, everywhere. Just open your eyes, open your awareness, and let the God in everything fill you."

It is time to normalize the sacred so that everything we do is a spiritual experience, from brushing our teeth to washing the dishes, from filling our car with gas to recycling household products, from making love to painting a picture, from seeing the magic in a baby's eyes to changing her diaper. There is no separation between us and God, between us and the sacred, except in our minds.

Resacralizing our lives means that everything we experience is imbued with sacredness. It means that we accept our sexuality as sacred, an expression of our divine nature. With this attitude we can greet our fellow humans as divine beings, Goddesses and Gods. We recognize the interconnectedness of all life and honor our Mother, the Earth, and all her creatures. When we normalize Sacred Sexuality, we will fully embrace each moment as an opportunity to experience ecstasy.

Chapter 28

Healing the Shame

The process of normalizing Sacred Sexuality involves examining our loss of innocence so that we can heal the shame, guilt, and fear of our past. It includes recognizing our woundedness, looking for the sacred gift in each experience, and forgiving ourselves and our abusers.

In my workshops on Sacred Sexuality participants reveal a myriad of examples of the shame, guilt, and fear instilled in them during their formative years. A young woman mentioned that when her mother told her about sex when she was eight years old, she felt totally disgusted and said, "Yuck! I will never do that!"

Her mother responded authoritatively, "You will. You have to. It's your duty!" This attitude of obligatory sex is responsible for many mentally and physically abusive situations.

A woman who had been married for thirty-seven years confided that only once had she made love with her eyes open. She said that it was the most profound lovemaking she and her husband had ever shared. She had been afraid to repeat the experience, feeling ashamed and unworthy of such ecstasy.

Another woman of forty-five said that each time she was pregnant with one of her four children, her mother would refuse to be seen with her in public because people would know her daughter had been doing it!

Recently when I asked my mother to spell the Dutch word, *gedoetje,* she was horrified. "You're not going to put that word in a book, are you? It's not nice!"

"Why?" I responded.

"Because it has to do with your ... you know ... your underneath."

Although my parents have mellowed in recent years, they have not changed their negative attitude toward the human body. Any form of nakedness is shameful to them. My dad was describing the health club which he recently joined. He stated, "Many of the men walk around naked in the dressing room. I hate it. It's ugly, ugly!"

Spiritual teacher Louise Hay says that most of us were brought up to believe in "Mama's God," a white-haired old man sitting on a cloud who watches our genitals to see if we do anything bad. Such fear of a wrathful God can condemn children to years of shame, guilt, and fear about their sexuality. There is an important difference between guilt and shame. Guilt is associated with our feelings about what we have done, while shame goes deeper to wound us with feelings about who we are. We are taught a hand-me-down shame that we are unworthy and sinful because we are sexual beings. Shame can even cause children to submit to repeated acts of abuse that they dare not expose for fear of being bad or losing the love of their abuser.

For most of us, our past experiences of sexuality contain shame, guilt, fear, and abuse. Fortunately, sexual and religious abuse have become subjects open for discussion. When we cease denying the abuse that has been occurring for thousands of years, we can break the cycle of abuse and heal our woundedness.

A woman named Sarah had uncovered through hypnotherapy that she had been sexually abused as a child. She was able to release the woundedness that she had buried for years in shame and denial. Sarah had been married for eleven years and had two children. She had always wondered why she felt so repulsed by sex. When she was able to heal her woundedness, she was free to release her body armoring and begin her journey of Sacred Sexuality.

Another woman expressed her rage at her father for abusing her as a young child. Through a healing process from Neuro-Linguistic Programming, she was able to retrieve her earliest experience of abuse. She visualized a conversation with her father in which she asked him why he had abused her. She understood his woundedness for the first time as he expressed that he had just wanted to feel loved. When she asked for the sacred gift in this experience, she realized that it had been a catalyst for growth, eventually leading to her inner journey back to wholeness.

A man named Ken shared the story of his abuse. When he was a choir boy in his Catholic Church, he always went to choir practice early because he loved singing and loved his church. One day before any of the other boys arrived, his priest sexually assaulted him. Ken's healing process has taken many years of dealing with the confusion and rage over being sexually abused by a man whom he looked upon as the representative of God. He was afraid to tell anyone what had happened because somehow he felt that he was guilty of causing the incident. His mother had recently written him a letter mentioning that Father Bob had been charged with sexually assaulting a young choir boy. Because the priest was not reported twenty years earlier, the cycle of abuse continued until someone had the courage to speak out.

Ken has found the sacred gift of his abuse. His healing process has led him to become a dynamic counselor who assists others in healing their woundedness.

A young woman who had been sexually abused as a teenager by an older, married man, spent years in dysfunctional relationships with men who were emotionally unavailable. Each of her partners reinforced her feelings of shame and low self-worth by being verbally abusive and by emotionally abandoning her. She was searching for someone to validate her, to fulfill her needs. In the process she gave away her soul to men who used her body, men who were incapable of loving her because they did not love themselves. She eventually began to work on her spiritual growth and rebuilt her self-esteem. Although she is now in a healthy relationship, she is afraid that she will lose her happiness and her lover because of the guilt and shame she still carries from her religious programming and from her abusive relationships. I recommended that she work with a therapist or a support group to help her heal her woundedness. She must continue her spiritual growth, or she will again expect her relationship to validate her, thus returning to her old pattern of codependence.

A call to action came from a fifty-year-old man who had recently discovered his path of Sacred Sexuality. He stated, "My biggest regret is that I taught my four children the same dysfunctional programming and hangups about sex that I received from my parents and they received from their parents. I did not stop the cycle of abuse. I beg those of you who have children, please, please stop the cycle now."

An example of a sexually healthy environment comes from an enlightened family which treats sexuality as sacred. There are two children, a boy, six, and a girl, four. When I asked the young parents how they are handling the subject of sexuality, the mother replied that she and her husband teach their children to respect the sacredness of their bodies. At age three her daughter reached up and pulled on her daddy's penis. He used this incident to teach the children boundaries, that everyone has a sacred, private body which must not be violated by others.

One morning she discovered her daughter crying and pointing to her brother's penis. "I wish I had one of those," she sobbed. This was the ideal opportunity for the mother to talk about the differences between female and male sex organs. Because sexuality is a subject that is discussed openly and in a sacred way, the parents are creating a trusting environment. Their children are bright and curious, unencumbered by shame and guilt programming. You can look into their eyes and see that they still remember who they are — they remember about God. Children who are free from shame, guilt, and fear programming will not have to go through the process of recovery from toxic beliefs. They will retain their curiosity and innocence, their spontaneity and exuberance for life.

The journey of Sacred Sexuality is a journey of healing and forgiveness. When we can take responsibility for all our choices, we are no longer a victim. Although we cannot change what happened in our past, we can change our perception of it. We can turn experiences of shame, guilt, and fear and experiences of abuse into our point of power. Our woundedness is our sacred teacher of love and forgiveness.

Choosing to accept the gift of our woundedness does *not* excuse the perverted behavior of our abusers. They are responsible for having committed a violation of our innocence. Although we forgive our abusers, we hold them responsible for their actions.

Chapter 29

Forgiving Our Parents

My parents have always chosen to act passionately on their convictions. Some of their beliefs are quite different from mine, and I have undergone an intense healing process to make peace with myself and with them. Dad is eighty-seven years old and still actively ministering to a small fundamentalist congregation. He preaches every Sunday, while Mom, who is eighty-nine, plays the piano in their church. She began taking piano lessons two years ago because their pianist had a stroke. They recently joined a health club and swim three days a week. Mom took swimming lessons because she had always been afraid of the water. Now she swims laps in the Olympic-size pool.

By the time *Do You Have an Owner's Manual for your Brain?* was published, I had spent many hours trying to decide how to tell my parents about my book. Out of respect for their religious beliefs, I had never told them that my path was different from theirs. Of course, my hidden agenda was my fear of the wrath of God in the form of their disapproval. I did not want to trigger any serious upset that might bring on Dad's heart problems or Mom's high blood pressure. I was afraid of any conflict between us. I never learned how to resolve conflict when I was growing up, just how to deny it. Any conflict in the family was immediately covered by Dad's singing of hymns. The more the conflict escalated, the more loudly he sang. "Amazing Grace" was his hymn of choice. He always won, and I learned to stuff my feelings.

My parents have mellowed in recent years. When their local newspaper interviewed me about *Do You Have an Owner's Manual for Your Brain?*, I described myself as a recovering fundamentalist Christian who had undergone an intense journey to overcome all the should's and should not's of my childhood. Although watching them read the article was hell, I had misjudged them. Mom said, "Why are you acting so nervous? This article is just like your book!"

That afternoon they supported me by coming to my booksigning. They keep an eye on the number of copies in their local bookstore and even request copies of the book from me for their friends.

On a recent visit I experienced the familiar identity crisis about ten minutes before arriving at their house. I thought, Who is going to visit my parents? Then I ran through the list of typical roles I had played: good little girl, wife, mother, people-pleaser, grown daughter. I realized I could no longer play a role. The answer came — my divine self is going to visit my parents. This insight brought a deep sense of peace and a freedom to express my love to Mom and Dad more fully.

All my experiences are the result of my choices. I do not blame my parents, although I feel hurt and sad that they did not teach me to cherish my body or honor my sexuality.

After I got married, Mom told me that she was frigid. She almost seemed proud of it and a bit disdainful of Dad's needs. What a role model! The passage of time has been good for their relationship, however. A few years ago she confided that they still have "lovie-dovie!"

223

My parents are my sacred teachers, and I honor their beautiful spirits. I love them deeply and am grateful for our close relationship. They are the hero and heroine of my life. "You must have a dream that is bigger than you," is Dad's advice to those who want to know the secret of his vibrancy and energy. Thank you, Mom and Dad. I am following your advice.

Δ Δ Δ

I used to feel angry and resentful toward my religion of origin because of the woundedness caused by my shame, guilt, and fear programming. It has taken years for me to forgive the religious abuse I experienced. Now I can comfortably visit my father's church and even sing the old hymns without pain. I play "Amazing Grace" on my native flute as a way to honor the fact that grace cannot be confined to one religion. Our beliefs are different, but the love is the same.

Have you forgiven your parents and your religion of origin? Have you forgiven those who abused you? Have you forgiven yourself? Regardless of the circumstances of your past, forgiveness will help to heal your woundedness. We cannot step fully onto our path of Sacred Sexuality until we forgive and release the ghosts of our past.

Chapter 30

Sex Talk

Sex, the most fearful and fascinating, the most guilt-ridden and ecstatic of arts, is a subject we do not discuss easily. Most of us have spent many years avoiding sex talk due to our shame, guilt, and fear programming. In order to share Sacred Sexuality, we must have the courage to communicate our innermost feelings, letting our partner know what we like and dislike. We are responsible for our own sexual satisfaction. We must have the courage to ask our partner for what we need in order to experience ecstasy.

How can we have healthy sex talk in our relationship? We must build trust and intimacy by getting in rapport. Rapport is the nonverbal aspect of sex talk that creates harmony and makes it comfortable for us to share our innermost feelings.

Matching your mate's breathing, body posture, movements, voice level and intensity, and primary communication system — visual, auditory, or kinesthetic — will help you get in rapport. It is the little things that communicate our love, from a gentle touch to a soul-searching glance; a thoughtful gesture to a cozy snuggle. Charlie and I like to get in rapport by holding each other while we are lying down, spoon fashion. As we lie quietly together, we synchronize our breathing and imagine that we are melting into each other. This form of rapport building is a bonding exercise that deepens trust and intimacy.

The four most terrifying words in a relationship are *We need to talk*. These words can cause our partner to shut down his emotions as a form of self-protection. He will either go into denial by stating, "There's nothing wrong;" or on the offensive, "You're always bugging me about our relationship;" or he will retreat into the television set. My greatest difficulty in our relationship used to be getting Charlie to express his emotions. He was raised to be the strong, silent male and has worked to overcome that pattern. I was programmed to be the people-pleasing female and used to talk too much, verbalizing before I had crystallized my thoughts. When Charlie expresses his emotions, as he does more easily now, his words are gifts of understanding for our relationship.

Sometimes when we are communicating something painful, we want to run away and hide from the rawness of our emotions. We can release the old reaction pattern of dancing away by staying present, processing through our impasse. In resisting the urge to run from conflict, ask yourself, What is the gift of this conflict? How can this experience be my sacred teacher?

The greatest challenge in sex talk and in relationship is to stay out of polarity. Polarity is the feeling of separateness, symbolized by the conflict between the sexes. That same conflict is a mirror of the inner conflict between our masculine and feminine energies. When we feel polarized, we become fearful and defensive and our ego takes control of our emotions. We create walls that separate us from the one we love the most. Many relationships die because the partners wait too long to communicate their feelings, particularly about their sex life. We can allow ourselves to be vulnerable, particularly in our sex talk. We release polarity as we become aware of our feelings of separateness and choose, instead, to create trust, harmony, and oneness.

Sex talk involves sharing your innermost feelings by revealing what you like and dislike about your sex life. In my workshops, we often demonstrate a way to share this information. One of our demos began with Charlie saying, "I like it when you initiate sex."

"I like it when you kiss me passionately at unexpected times, not just during our lovemaking."

Charlie and I were illustrating a sex-talk exercise in front of a group of forty-five people. The process consists of a round — a like, dislike, and then a like from each partner. When we hear something that is painful, we do not respond verbally. We discuss our feelings immediately afterward, but the exercise should continue without distraction for as many rounds as are agreed upon at the beginning.

"I don't like it when you are not mentally present during sex."

Charlie's statement was true but painful to hear. I took a deep breath and continued. "I don't like it when you are goal oriented."

"I like making love at unexpected times and places."

It was my turn to speak, and I was thinking about how much I enjoy oral sex. I felt my words getting tangled in a right-brain processing. "I like ... I like it ... I like your tongue!"

The group and I broke into nervous laughter. The old reaction pattern of shame had sneaked into my expression. Because of this incident it has become much easier to say in front of a group, "I love it when we share oral sex." It was a healing experience for me to struggle with breaking the old pattern of shame.

The next day I received a note from one of the workshop participants. It said, "Dear Marina, Thank you for your gift of talking about oral sex. I had always felt guilty when my husband, Rick, tried to get me to make love in this way. I could do it for him, but my religious programming of shame taught me that nice girls didn't receive oral sex. Your statement last night was a healing for me. It gave me permission to fully enjoy my sexuality and Rick's tongue!" It was signed, "Love, Anne."

We must stop the guessing game about what we do and do not like in our sexual relationship with our mate. Another healing method of communicating our feelings is to play the "I Feel" game. Take turns making the following statements to each other: "I feel scared when ... I feel angry when ... I feel abandoned when ... I feel sad when ... I feel happy when ... I feel ecstasy when ..." This exercise empowers couples to take responsibility for their emotions. Do not accept a statement that begins, "You make me feel ..." No one can make us feel any emotion without our permission.

Sex talk requires a beginner's mind. A beginner's mind focuses on the present and sees the beloved as brand new in each moment. We have a tendency to replay all our old dramas, dragging our past into the present. While it is important to heal and release our woundedness, communication can easily reach an impasse when we replay all the old resentments we have felt toward each other. If you feel stuck in your sex talk, ask yourself, Is this the truth about my beloved? Is what I am feeling the truth about who we really are?

Our sex talk will be enhanced when we realize that every action is a request for love. No matter how hurtful the comment your mate makes, he is really asking, Do you love me? If we approach every communication as a request for love, we will be able to heal our relationships.

In traveling around the United States and the world, I am constantly reminded of how many lonely people there are. In one of the churches where I spoke, a four-year-old boy and his mother were visiting for the first time. After the service was over, the little boy watched as people hugged each other. He spoke loudly, "Isn't there someone here I can love?" A man standing nearby heard his question and held out his arms. The little boy ran to him, thrilled to be shown affection. We are all like that little boy, wondering how we can give and receive the love that we crave.

Sex talk involves trust and intimacy; releasing polarity; sharing your innermost feelings, including your sexual likes and dislikes; and maintaining a beginner's mind. When we can communicate our needs with our beloved, we will be sharing conscious loving and enhancing our experience of Sacred Sexuality.

Chapter 31

The Inner Soulmate

I met Francisco, an Apache warrior, in Ouray, Colorado. He was managing his nephew's shop where Charlie and I stopped to browse and examine the exquisite Native American jewelry. When I looked into Francisco's eyes, I felt an immediate heart connection with him. I intuitively knew that he had something important to share with us. We began asking him questions about his native spirituality, and soon we were engrossed in conversation. Francisco shared his traditions with us, stopping occasionally to answer a customer's question or complete a sale. Three hours passed rapidly. As we prepared to leave, Francisco took Charlie's hand, and placing it in mine, he said, "Listen to her, for she will lead you."

As Charlie and I continued our exploration of Ouray, we discussed what Francisco had shared with us. At the time neither of us fully comprehended the meaning of his parting statement. This experience occurred shortly after we had moved to Colorado. It took years for the meaning of Francisco's wisdom to become clear. He was speaking symbolically when he placed Charlie's hand in mine. He was indicating that our masculine energy would be led by our feminine energy to return to a place of balance. Each of us has a dual nature represented by our inner masculine and inner feminine energies. These energies are often imbalanced or at war with each other.

Francisco was saying that our inner man, our logical, assertive, left-brain side, must listen to and be willing to be led by our inner woman, which is our intuitive, feeling, right-brain side. The masculine principle has dominated the course of history for over six thousand years, leading our species and all life on our planet to the brink of destruction. It is time for our feminine energy to lead us to a place of harmony within ourselves and within our relationship with our mate. It is also our feminine energy that will lead us to create harmony in our relationship with Mother Earth and all her creatures.

Δ Δ Δ

Many of us have projected our inner man or inner woman onto our mate. Instead of seeking fulfillment in connecting with our Inner Soulmate, we fall into the trap of romantic projection and expect our mate to complete us and fulfill our every expectation. Even the dictionary struggles with the definition of romance. Synonyms like adventure and idealization seem inappropriate but understandable. One dictionary definition is "Love ... a strong, usually short-lived attachment or enthusiasm." Romantic love as the basis for marriage has been around for only 150 years. It is based on projection and keeps us stuck in codependence. We project our idealized expectations of the perfect God-man or Goddess-woman onto our mate. When our other half disappoints us, we begin searching for someone else who will complete us. They never will. Two halves never will make a whole person — they will make a codependent relationship of two imbalanced, needy people.

In my workshops, I lead participants through an exercise to connect with their Inner Soulmate, which is the sacred marriage of their inner woman and inner man. Participants usually visualize their inner woman quite easily. It is much more challenging for them to access their inner man. The images are often fuzzy, if they show up at all. I believe this is because we have had few models of balanced masculine energy. Many of us have been abused by masculine energy that is out of balance and out of control.

We find the balance of our dual nature as we connect with our Inner Soulmate. I was meditating on this balance when I decided to ask for total, instant enlightenment. I was feeling impatient with the seeming slowness of my inner journey. We were staying at an RV park on the beach in Gulf Shores, Alabama. It was during an afternoon meditation that I requested that every cell in my body be fully enlightened. After my meditation, I walked to the fishing pier a half mile away to see what Charlie had caught. Rather than fishing, he was standing at the end of the pier with a group of people. He motioned for me to come quickly. One of the men had hooked a large shark, and several other men were trying to get it into a big landing net which they had lowered into the water. Each time the men almost netted the shark, it slipped away. It was fighting hard to resist the net. Whenever I am on a fishing pier, I always send energy to the fish. I whispered to the shark, "You can get free. You can get free." Ten minutes later the men netted the shark and pulled it up onto the pier. It was about four and a half feet long. It flopped out of the net, and one of the men slipped the hook out of its gill as easily as slipping an earring wire out of a pierced ear. That was the first lesson of the shark — what you resist, persists. If the shark had released instead of struggling so hard, it would have been free.

Charlie told me that it was illegal to catch sharks off the pier and it would have to be thrown back. What happened instead was a brutal, shocking sight. The fisherman who had hooked the shark, a tall, burly man, grabbed the shark by the tail with both hands. He slung it around his head twice and then clubbed the shark's head on the pier as hard as he could. The sound was a sickening "whomp" that reverberated through my body. What had begun as a curious incident had turned into a brutal execution. Shocked and horrified, I ran away from the scene, tears blurring my vision. Before I got off the pier, I heard and felt another whomp. I screamed, "No! No! No!" as I ran down the deserted beach to our motor home.

I sobbed as I relived the cruelty of this act of violence. There was no evidence that the fisherman recognized the importance of giving thanks to the spirit of the shark, asking for permission to take its life, as is the Native American custom. "He never even asked permission," I sobbed over and over. Although I was exhausted from the intensity of my emotions, I knew I needed to do a ceremony to honor the spirit of the shark. I took my drum and rattle to the beach and chanted and prayed to release its spirit into the next dimension.

I meditated on this incident over the next three days. I had requested total enlightenment, and instead, I had witnessed a brutal execution. How were the two events related? The answer came during my meditation on the third day. Shark energy is masculine energy because it is an aggressive, predator fish. The fisherman also represented masculine energy that is completely out of balance from its feminine counterpart. As I viewed the incident on the pier, I represented feminine energy. I was unable to stay present at the scene — I ran away. For six thousand years, feminine energy has run away from the cruelty and domination of imbalanced masculine energy. Feminine energy in both women and men can no longer run away from the violence of imbalanced masculine energy. We must stay present to heal our inner masculine. I am speaking metaphorically. I am not saying to stay in an abusive relationship.

We must stop running away from ourselves. We are not separate from the shark and the fisherman. They are symbols of our masculine energy when it is out of balance. We must bring balance back into the relationship of our polarized masculine and feminine energies. It is through the heroic journey into the self that we unite these energies in our Inner Soulmate.

Chapter 32

Ecstasy!

Tuning in to the rhythm of the ocean both calms and excites me. Yesterday it was a lake of glass, the calmness of a deep meditation reflecting the presence of eternity. Last night a frontal system from the Southwest brought heavy rain and high wind, transforming the ocean into a churning tempest. As I walk along the beach, the waves rush up to meet my bare feet with a warm greeting, fingers of foam tickling my ankles. I experience ecstasy when I face the waves and feel them crashing on the shore. They are a part of me, an expression of wild creativity and the depth of passion that flows through me.

It is scary to end this book. People have asked me how I know when a book is finished. That is like asking a woman how she knows when her baby is ready to be born. It is a feeling of fullness, of completion. My book has become my friend, my constant companion. Letting go is difficult.

This book has been my story of awakening to ecstasy, which is a state of mind, body, and spirit that takes us out of the ordinary. It is a sense of communing with the Goddesses and Gods who represent humanity's origin and destination. Ecstasy is moving beyond polarity into oneness. We can experience ecstasy at any moment

— during a walk on the beach or while emptying the garbage; during meditation or while stopped at a traffic light; during lovemaking or while paying bills. We experience ecstasy when we embrace life fully, when we become who we really are. It is that moment when the veil between us and our divinity lifts and we know ourselves as one with the ocean, the garbage, the traffic, our lover, and our money.

Each person's experience of ecstasy is unique. You recognize it when you feel your edges slipping away, when there is no more separation between you and your beloved, between you and all life forms. I identify ecstasy by a tingling feeling that moves up my spine, a sense of energy vibrating in my body. The world looks sharper, cleaner, and brighter, with an intensity that makes me feel like crying. At other times my surroundings take on the soft focus of dream imagery in which time and space seem to melt together into an eternal now.

Sacred Sexuality opens the door to an ever deepening experience of ecstasy. My daily practice of Sacred Sexuality exercises has led to an awareness of the movement of sexual energy in my body and in my relationship with my beloved. We have expanded our awareness of the sensuality of touch, breath, movement, and sound in sharing our bodies and souls in a dance of ecstasy.

Δ Δ Δ

My writing of this book began in the mountains of Colorado. Nestled in my canyon retreat, surrounded by rugged cliffs and the winged ones, I was able to process the sexual experiences of my past in an environment that offered healing and inspiration. I have completed this book while on tour, giving talks, workshops, and seminars to thousands of people across the United States and around the world. Many of these people have touched my life with the intensity of their journey. Their willingness to question old patterns, heal their woundedness, and undertake their journey of Sacred

Sexuality has been an inspiration. If we wish to awaken to ecstasy, we can no longer remain stuck in conformity to old patterns. It takes trust and courage to transform our lives. We must release our attachment to the security of who we used to be, embrace the unknown, and find harmony with our Inner Soulmate. The journey of Sacred Sexuality is our invitation to ecstasy.

It was also during my writing of this book that my cat, Jopie, age nineteen, made his transition. He spent many of my writing hours curled up in my lap, loving me while I loved each chapter into existence. He was my teacher of unconditional love, wisdom, and dignity. He passed away in my arms, looking deeply into my soul. His energy is a part of this book. I love you, Jopie.

Last fall Charlie and I visited Sedona, Arizona, where we met a Native American medicine man. I felt an immediate heart connection with Grandfather. I asked him to recommend a place of power where I could go to meditate. Sedona is known for its energy vortexes that are sacred sites to many people. Grandfather looked deeply into my eyes and ceremoniously pointed his finger toward my heart. "Right there," he said. "Wherever you take that — that is your place of power."

We are being called to be in our place of power. In order to heal our woundedness and experience Sacred Sexuality, we must listen to the gentle voice of our heart. That voice calls us to connect with our Inner Soulmate, to awaken to our ecstasy.

I wish you love, joy, peace, and ecstasy on your journey of Sacred Sexuality. In the words of a Native American benediction, "May you walk consciously on the Earth. May every movement you make have purpose, every word you speak have meaning, and every thought be a prayer. Aho. Mitakuye Oyasin."

The Beginning ...

Appendix I
Breaking the Cycle
of Abuse

How do we break the cycle of abuse that has led to our psychosexual woundedness? We begin by releasing the shame, guilt, and fear that has separated us from the sacredness of our bodies and our sexuality. We must educate our children from birth about the sanctity of the human body, teaching them to honor their sexuality as a sacred gift.

We need courageous women and men to share their stories so that we may learn from their experiences and their healing process. We allow ourselves to be vulnerable by telling the truth about our past, yet we do not do so from a victim mentality. We can heal our woundedness when we look upon each experience as our sacred teacher.

Women need to awaken to their power to create their lives without the burden of shame, guilt, and fear. When we value our bodies and our sexuality as sacred, we can experience lovemaking as a holy sacrament. The women's spirituality movement is providing many of my sisters with the loving support of a group of like-minded women. It has also birthed the eco-feminist movement, which is awakening us to our responsibility to love, respect, and care for our Mother, the Earth, and all her creatures.

We need men to recognize their feminine energy and reconnect with their hearts. Whether we refer to this as their deep masculine or inner feminine, the results are the same. The men's movement is giving men an opportunity to get back in touch with their emotions, to rediscover their hearts. I am encouraged by the number of men who are opening themselves to a fuller, more balanced expression of their essence, their Inner Soulmate. When women and men choose to experience their sexuality as sacred, they will walk in harmony and balance on the Earth.

Δ Δ Δ

Many of us have suffered deeply as a result of the programming of salvation psychology. Awareness of the abusive effects of shame, guilt, and fear programming is spreading. More and more individuals are empowering themselves and releasing their toxic beliefs. The following is my comparison of the precepts of Salvation Psychology and Sacred Sexuality:

Precepts of Salvation Psychology	Precepts of Sacred Sexuality
1. God is a white male who is to be feared and obeyed.	1. God is a loving Spirit, neither male nor female.
2. Man has dominion over the earth, to rule and subdue it.	2. The Earth is a living entity, our Mother. She feeds, clothes, and houses us.
3. Women are inferior to men. The Bible states that God took a rib from Adam to create Eve. (This totally reverses the natural order of the birth cycle.)	3. Women and men are equals, both embodying feminine and masculine energy. We are all spiritual beings having a human experience.
4. Women's purpose in life is to serve men. The Biblical words are, "Wives, submit unto your husbands."	4. Women are powerful beings who are serving as healers to return balance to our Earth family.
5. Men are the spiritual head of the family.	5. Men are awakening to the harmony of their Inner Soulmate.

6. Homosexuals are an abomination in the eyes of God.

6. Divine Spirit is free of judgment. All sexual preferences can lead to Sacred Sexuality.

7. Babies are born into the world as evil, sinful beings.

7. Babies are born spiritually whole. They are expressions of Divine Spirit.

8. The human body is shameful, especially the genitals.

8. The human body is sacred, the temple of the Divine.

9. Sex is dirty and sinful. Our sexuality is evidence of our evil nature.

9. Sex is a precious, sacred gift, a doorway to oneness with the Divine.

10. Anyone who has been abused is a victim of their abuser's sinful and perverted nature.

10. There are no victims. Our woundedness is our sacred teacher of love and forgiveness.

11. Because of the original sin of Adam and Eve, we are all destined to suffer while on the earth. Our only hope is to confess our sins and be saved so that we can go to heaven.

11. We deserve ecstasy. It is our birthright. We are on the planet to live joyously. When we understand that every moment is sacred, we can create heaven on Earth.

Nothing short of a spiritual/sexual revolution is going to stop the cycle of abuse. The answers do not come from outside ourselves, from holy books written by men hundreds of years ago. We will find our answers within the sacred gifts of our experiences. I hope that the story of my sexual healing and awakening to ecstasy will serve as encouragement on your journey of Sacred Sexuality.

We must look within and recapture our dreams of our possible future. If we do not change, we will destroy our species. We are on the threshold of the quantum leap in consciousness that will transform life as we know it. It is time to reawaken to ecstasy, time to embrace our Sacred Sexuality.

Appendix II
Action Steps to Healing

Many people ask me what they can do to heal their woundedness. My greatest healing has come from changing my perception of my woundedness and understanding it as my sacred teacher of love and forgiveness. The journey of Sacred Sexuality will awaken you to your wholeness. An immediate step involves writing the answers to the following questions:

1. What are my deepest wounds?
2. Do I consider myself a victim?
3. What has been my pay-off for being a victim? (We get sympathy; we indulge in self-pity; we can blame our problems on our abuser.)
4. Do I love myself?
5. Have I forgiven myself?
6. Have I forgiven my abusers?
7. Am I willing to learn the lessons of my woundedness?
8. How would I be empowered by perceiving my woundedness as a sacred gift?
9. What is the gift of my woundedness?
10. How can it be a catalyst for my growth?
11. Am I willing to heal my woundedness?
12. How will my life change when I heal my woundedness?
13. How will releasing my programming of shame, guilt, and fear affect my feelings about myself and my sexuality?
14. How will the journey of Sacred Sexuality transform my life?
15. Am I willing to accept ecstasy?

The following action steps are important to the process of healing your woundedness:

1. Go to a psychotherapist. There are many forms of therapy to choose from. A practitioner who utilizes Neuro-Linguistic Programming can help you to process your experiences through short-term therapy.
2. Get bodywork to help release the cellular memory of your abuse. Massage, Reiki, Jin Shin Jyutsu, and energy work have all been helpful in my healing.
3. Join a support group such as *A Course in Miracles,* a women's or a men's group, or a progressive church that teaches love, not fear, e.g., Unity Church of Christianity or Church of Religious Science.
4. Keep a journal of your healing journey. Reading about your growth will encourage you when you feel stuck.
5. Explore the sacredness of your sexuality by committing at least one night a week to enjoying sacred sexual practices.
6. Share the story of your healing with others. By sharing what you have experienced, you will empower yourself and others.
7. Exercise daily. It is a must for creating harmony of body, mind, and spirit.
8. Spend time in nature. Allow Mother Earth and her creatures to teach you about the sacredness of all life.
9. Take time to breathe deeply, to laugh, and to dream. Savor the ecstasy in each moment.

Everything comes to us at the right time. Therefore, it is no accident that you have read this book. You are ready to enter a new dimension of wholeness. You are a sacred, sexual being with a special mission on the planet. May your journey of Sacred Sexuality bring you love, joy, peace, and ecstasy.

Sexuality: The Sacred Journey
Quotes

Chapter 3: People who surrender their free will and act from blind obedience violate the integrity of the soul.

Awareness is the first step in any healing process.

Disease always has a reason, although the reason is usually unconscious.

You can choose to change your perception of your woundedness and look upon each experience as a sacred teacher.

Chapter 5: We will experience healing when we accept the lesson in every painful event.

Chapter 7: The journey into the self leads us to abandon the security of the predictable life, charting our path into the high mountainous territory of our soul.

Chapter 8: It is time for a new model of relationship that is based on a sacred partnership between two whole, self-actualized individuals.

Chapter 9: When we can embrace all our experiences, even the most painful, as our sacred teachers, we empower ourselves.

Chapter 10: Without open, honest communication, a relationship will die, strangled by distrust and fear.

Chapter 12: The fallacy of romantic love is that through projecting our ideal of perfection onto the object of our love, we empower that person to control our happiness.

Chapter 13: Sex without love causes deep wounding at the soul level.

When we stop judging ourselves as guilty, we allow our journey of Sacred Sexuality to unfold.

Chapter 14: Everything happens for a reason. We draw people and events to us so that we may learn valuable lessons from them.

When we choose to abuse ourselves, we will find someone willing to help us administer the punishment.

Religious programming of shame, guilt, and fear has its strongest hold on us through our sexual relationships.

Chapter 18: Never avoid feeling stuck. It is always the prelude to true understanding.

It is impossible to run away from our fears. They will continue to haunt us until we receive their gifts.

Chapter 19: Our cultural conditioning has taught women to be the projection of a man's soul, of his inner feminine, by being placed on a pedestal and playing the part of the idealized woman.

It is the ultimate journey to retrieve our soul from its projection onto our other half. This sacred journey reunites us with our Inner Soulmate, the harmony of our feminine and masculine energies.

There is a wild, untamed aspect of each of us that represents our raw, sexual energy. We are programmed to feel shame, guilt, and fear when we experience this source of power.

The journey of Sacred Sexuality allows us to release our protective armoring, opening us to our capacity for wholeness and for ecstasy.

Chapter 20: Being able to relax and enjoy being happy can be difficult if you were programmed to believe that you should suffer.

We are here to increase our capacity to love and forgive.

The journey of Sacred Sexuality challenges us to break down the walls of fear and share ourselves in trust and vulnerability.

Chapter 21: We are totally responsible for our own sexual pleasure and fulfillment.

When we think of life as a sacred circle, then there is no linear progression. All paths lead to truth.

A relationship works when we stop projecting our expectations onto our mate.

Being spiritual does not mean that we have to deny our bodies.

We are creatures of habit, and even pain is often more comfortable than the risk of the unknown.

We are pioneers building models of loving relationships that celebrate the sacredness of sexuality and the sacredness of all life.

Chapter 22: Each of us needs to experience a return to innocence, the innocence that we had as babies before the process of negative conditioning and abuse began to cloud our perception of ourselves as sacred, sexual beings.

Our relationship with the entire world changes when we replace shame with pride, guilt with innocence, and fear with courage.

Chapter 24: When we are one with the sacredness of all life, every moment is sacred.

Chapter 26: The greatest challenge to men is to be present with their emotions ... I urge my brothers to do whatever is necessary to open themselves to their deepest emotions and express them unashamedly.

Chapter 27: Fear can be our sacred teacher if we confront it and work our way through it.

If you don't change, you will be a victim of your own history.

There is no separation between us and God, between us and the sacred, except in our minds.

Chapter 28: We are taught a hand-me-down shame that we are unworthy and sinful because we are sexual beings.

Children who are free from shame, guilt, and fear programming will not have to go through the process of recovery from toxic beliefs.

Chapter 29: You must have a dream that is bigger than you.

... grace cannot be confined to one religion. Our beliefs are different, but the love is the same.

Regardless of the circumstances of your past, forgiveness will help to heal your woundedness.

Chapter 30: We must have the courage to ask our partner for what we need in order to experience ecstasy.

The four most terrifying words in a relationship are *We need to talk.*

We release polarity as we become aware of our feelings of separateness and choose, instead, to create trust, harmony, and oneness.

A beginner's mind focuses on the present and sees the beloved as brand new in each moment.

If we approach every communication as a request for love, we will be able to heal our relationships.

Chapter 31: We must stop running away from ourselves.

We must bring balance back into the relationship of our polarized masculine and feminine energies.

Chapter 32: Ecstasy is a state of mind, body, and spirit that takes us out of the ordinary.

Ecstasy is moving beyond polarity into oneness. It is a feeling of being at one with all of life.

The journey of Sacred Sexuality is our invitation to ecstasy.

In order to heal our woundedness and awaken to Sacred Sexuality, we must listen to the gentle voice of our heart.

"May you walk consciously on the Earth. Aho. Mitakuye Oyasin."

Appendix I: We must educate children from birth about the sanctity of the human body and teach them to honor their sexuality as a sacred gift.

We will find our answers within the sacred gifts of our experiences.

We are on the threshold of the quantum leap in consciousness that will transform life as we know it.

About the Artist

Charles Frizzell is a gentle spirit who lives high in the Colorado mountains. His images are inspired by his love of nature, his dreams, and his passion for the sacredness of all life.

His work is available in limited edition prints, art posters, originals, calenders, and greeting cards. I consider him to be the foremost visionary artist in the world. He is my friend and I love him.

For information on Frizzell art contact:

Frizzell Studios
P.O. Box 495
Victor, CO 80860
(719) 689-2232

Sacred
Sexuality Adventure
3-Day Weekend Workshop

Free yourself from the shame, guilt, and fear programming, while gaining tools for deepening your capacity for ecstasy. Celebrate the sacredness of life in a weekend workshop with Marina Raye and Charlie Oakwind.

- Learn keys to enrich your sex life
- Release sexual guilt and shame
- Connect with your Inner Soulmate
- Harmonize intimacy and passion
- Intensify sacred sexual expression
- Explore the magic of Tantric love

This training will lead you into a deeper understanding of yourself and your journey of Sacred Sexuality. Designed for individuals and couples, you will learn a new language of intimacy through Sacred Sexuality practices. Understand your woundedness as a sacred gift. Release your past sexual programming through NLP and holographic healing.

These exciting weekend workshops are held in Colorado and other locations. If you would like to receive workshop announcements, please send your name and address to:

Action Press
P.O. Box 6250
Colorado Springs, CO 80934
719-577-9577

If your organization would like to sponsor a **Sacred Sexuality Adventure** weekend, please contact Action Press.

A Weekend of Pure Ecstasy

Do You Have an
Owner's Manual for Your Brain?
by
Marina Raye

"A parable for our time. Gives much to think about and use on your own path of enlightenment."
Dr. Wayne W. Dyer, author of *Real Magic*

Do You Have an Owner's Manual for Your Brain?

Marina Raye takes you on a magical journey of self-discovery in a transformational book that is science faction. Maya Cristal is an advanced soul living in Chichen Itza, Mexico, during the Classical Mayan Period. She is chosen for the mission of bringing the *Owner's Manual* to 21st Century Earthlings.

Maya will awaken you to a deeper understanding of yourself and your higher purpose. It is Maya who leads us beyond the path of technology to the path of the heart by bringing a gift to each of us — the gift of ourselves.

Δ Δ Δ

- Gain tools to make your brain user-friendly
- Access greater personal power
- Enhance your relationships
- Live with peace of mind
- Choose healing and total wellness
- Rediscover your creativity
- Take an active role in the return to ecobalance

"... a galvanizing good read that will draw you back a second and third time to dig for self-help gold once you've enjoyed the fascinating, futuristic story."
***Better World* Magazine**

"A timely message — one that will touch your heart and expand your world, stretching your mind around new corners." **Thea Alexander,** author of *2150 A.D.*

"I feel that this book is a much needed help to those on the planet that wish to grow to full spiritual power." **Sun Bear, Medicine Chief,** author of *Black Dawn, Bright Day*

"A feast of images, feelings, and ideas to nourish the soul in practical ways!" **Rev. Edie Skalitzky,** Unity Minister and Seminar Leader

"A colorful adventure of consciousness, *Owner's Manual* offers a clear and positive blueprint for successful living and a healed planet — a book with heart." **Alan Cohen,** author of *Joy Is My Compass*

"The author is clearly one of the most positive, active people on the planet." ***Better World* Magazine**

ISBN 1-878010-00-X $12.95
Trade Paperback 320 pages
Available through your local bookstore or from
Action Press. Please use order form on page 255.

Brainware: The Workbook

The accompanying guide to *Do You Have an Owner's Manual for Your Brain?* in an easy-to-use workbook format. Powerful tools and visualizations to assist your transformational journey with user-friendly software for your brain. *Brainware* will help you to:

- Find and live your mission
- Gain an understanding of NLP communication skills
- Choose new blueprints while releasing fear
- Access your creativity
- Choose high-level wellness
- Live consciously on Mother Earth
- Utilize Native American ceremony
- Make life a passionate adventure

130 pages $12.95
(Please use order form on page 255.)

The Vision

When we fearlessly bring the message of Sacred Sexuality into the light of the new day, we will transform our lives and give birth to a new world that is free from shame, guilt, and fear.

Marina Raye welcomes your comments about how
Sexuality: The Sacred Journey has touched your life.
Address correspondence to:

Marina Raye c/o Action Press,
P.O. Box 6250
Colorado Springs, CO 80934

719-577-9577

Coming soon from Action Press
Sacred Sexuality: The Workbook
by
Marina Raye